They Call Me
Orange Juice

Audrey Adems

They Call Me
Orange Juice

Stories and Essays

Audrey McDonald Atkins

ARCHWAY
PUBLISHING

This book is a work of non-fiction. Unless otherwise noted, the author and the publisher make no explicit guarantees as to the accuracy of the information contained in this book and in some cases, names of people and places have been altered to protect their privacy.

Archway Publishing books may be ordered through booksellers or by contacting:

Archway Publishing
1663 Liberty Drive
Bloomington, IN 47403
www.archwaypublishing.com
1 (888) 242-5904

Because of the dynamic nature of the Internet, any web addresses or links contained in this book may have changed since publication and may no longer be valid. The views expressed in this work are solely those of the author and do not necessarily reflect the views of the publisher, and the publisher hereby disclaims any responsibility for them.

Any people depicted in stock imagery provided by Getty Images are models, and such images are being used for illustrative purposes only.
Certain stock imagery © Getty Images.

Interior Image Credit: Maya Metz Logue

ISBN: 978-1-4808-5941-8 (sc)
ISBN: 978-1-4808-5940-1 (hc)
ISBN: 978-1-4808-5942-5 (e)

Library of Congress Control Number: 2018903831

Print information available on the last page.

Archway Publishing rev. date: 4/19/2018

For Ricky and Darby Jack

Contents

Introduction

Storytelling runs in my family.

We sit around and tell the same tales over and over and over. Somehow, they never get old. Extra emphasis, a rolled eye, a dramatic pause entertains. A little extra detail here and there educates. In the retelling, heritage and history are passed down.

My grandfather, "Baw" to me, and his brothers hear someone is coming to visit driving a fancy, new car. Mischievous young'uns, they conspire to put nails out in the dirt road in hopes that the car will get a flat, and they a closer look.

Granny's grandparents make a journey to Colorado hoping for a better life. They tie a rope between their home and the outhouse so that they can find their way back and forth in the blinding snow. After a hard year in the mountains, they return home to south Alabama, wiser.

Daddy and his brothers, boys who dive down, down, down to the bottom of one of the pilings that holds up the railroad trestle where it crosses the river. There's an opening, and they swim up inside the piling, up, up, up, until there is an air pocket.

Mama reciting my hometown's family trees for generations and generations back. Who is related to whom. Where they came from. Where they went. What they did.

> Five little fishes swimming in a brook. Papa caught 'em with a hook.

Mama fried 'em in a pan.
Daddy ate 'em like a man.
I snuck in to get a bite, and Daddy knocked me outta
sight!

Uncle Red's singsongy poem, complete with a roundhouse punch at the end, told to a giggling little towheaded girl over and over and over.

All my life, these stories and so many more were told on a dark, summer front porch, around the fireplace, over the dinner table. And when I was old enough, I chimed in with my stories too. I didn't have a lot of history to share, but I quickly learned that I could make people laugh. I knew it was a really good one if Mama laughed so hard she wheezed.

That's why I started to write. That's why I started my blog, Folkways Nowadays (folkwaysnowadays.com). I had some extra time on my hands and a head full of stories I wanted to tell.

The first story started with a blank screen. I wrote it out thinking Mama would read it and, I hoped, like it. That's what Mamas are for. Maybe a few of my friends would read too. Maybe.

Mama did like it.

So I kept on writing.

A few friends did read.

So I kept on writing.

A few more folks read.

So I kept on writing.

Now, I've written so many little stories and little essays that here I am with a little book.

However, before I ever had a blog, before I ever had a book, I was a storyteller—a storyteller from a long line of storytellers. And a story-teller I shall remain, for as long as there are stories to tell.

For as long as you'll keep on reading them.

The Dark Blot

I like to say that I was raised BaptistMethodistEpiscopalHoliness with a little dash of Church of God thrown in for good measure. As the daughter of Episcopalian parents with Baptist and Methodist grandparents, Holiness friends, and Church of God help, religion was always close at hand. In a town as small as Citronelle, Alabama, there wasn't much else to *do* except go to church—somebody's church, anybody's church, whichever church was having something.

We went to fish fries, Christmas bazaars, covered-dish dinners, dinners on the ground, revivals (both inside buildings and under tents), singings, camp meetings, and vacation Bible school. It was a social outlet with the added perk of eternal salvation. At times, however, I found myself somewhat conflicted.

You see, there weren't very many Episcopalians in Citronelle. We might have had fourteen worshipers on a good Sunday, and our family made up four of them. There certainly weren't enough young'uns to have any sort of consistent Sunday school program, so I went to Sunday school at the First Baptist Church, where Granny (and my best friend) was a member. We learned all the good stories—Samson and Delilah, David and Goliath, Jonah and the whale—and the concomitant moral lessons, all washed down with a lukewarm glass of grape Kool-Aid and an Oreo.

After Sunday school was "big church," the eleven o'clock service, which was an hour-plus of sweating, pulpit pounding, hoarse hollering, and hellfire raining down on our collective heads to be endured along with hunger pangs no Starlight mint could assuage. I always knew the end was near when the pianist would start softly playing "Just As I Am," but that also meant my weekly internal battle was about to be waged.

As the preacher would slowly and meaningfully descend the sea foam green, carpeted steps to stand among us sinners, the congregants would rise to meet him, quietly beginning to sing the first of six verses.

> ♫ Just as I am without one plea, but that thy blood was
> shed for thee, and that thou biddest me come to thee,
> O Lamb of God, I come, I come … ♪

The preacher would start to beseech the lost to come up and accept Jesus as their Lord and Savior, and I would wonder if I had the call or if I was just hungry. What if I had the call but just wasn't recognizing it? Was I going to hell? Could it wait until next Sunday so I could see if I was sure? *Oh dang! Next Sunday we're going to the Methodist church for family day.*

> ♫ Just as I am, and waiting not, to rid my soul of one
> dark blot; to Thee whose blood can cleanse each spot,
> O Lamb of God, I come, I come … ♪

A dark blot? I have a dark blot? I did lie to my mama when I said my stomach hurt too bad to go to school. Shoot! I've gone and given myself the dark blot of a sinner! I'm sure to burn in hell! I'd better go down. I'd better confess it all. I'd better fall to my very knees and pray for forgiveness from the One who can cleanse this horrible spot!

> ♫ Just as I am, though tossed about, with many a con-
> flict, many a doubt; fightings within, and fears with-
> out, O Lamb of God, I come, I come … ♪

Wait a minute. If I go down to the altar, will that make me Baptist? I'm supposed to be Episcopalian. Can Episcopalians even *go* down there?

I'll be at St. Thomas this afternoon anyway with my parents. I'll just bet I can have this whole dark-blot problem sewn up then. Yes. Yes! I have "done those things which I ought not to have done!" Good old *Book of Common Prayer.* I can handle this whole blot thing without having to expose myself as a sinner to this whole sanctuary of people who already think I'm a little weird and different because I'm not really one of them. Thank you, Lord! Now if I can just live until four o'clock.

♫ Just as I am, poor, wretched, blind; sight, riches, healing of the mind; yes, all I need, in Thee to find, O Lamb of God, I come, I come ... ♪

All right, folks, let's wrap this service up now. It's twelve fifteen, and Mama is making crabmeat casserole for lunch. All *I* need now is to get on home. Wait just a minute! Who is that woman headed to the altar? Couldn't she have gotten the call during the first verse? We're almost to the end. We were so close! Did I just sin? Is it a sin to want to deny somebody his or her eternal peace and salvation because you're nearly starved to death? Maybe I really am wretched! Maybe I'm just delirious with hunger. I'll fix this at four too.

♫ Just as I am, Thou wilt receive, wilt welcome, pardon, cleanse, relieve; because thy promise I believe, O Lamb of God, I come, I come ... ♪

Okay, that was fast. She prayed. She cried. She's headed back to her pew to lean weakly on her husband, emotionally spent and somewhat sweaty. Whew! That was close! What's this? The preacher is heading back up the minty stairs! We're almost in the clear. We and our souls are in the heavenly homestretch!

Amen!

We Say Grace

We say grace.

Here in the Bible Belt, rarely a meal starts without someone saying grace—a prayer of devotion and gratitude—before the family dives in. We give thanks for the nourishment of our bodies and souls. We give thanks for the blessing of another day. We give thanks for family and friends.

Grace can take many forms. As children, we recited the singsongy:

> God is great.
> God is good.
> Let us thank Him for our food.
> By His hands we all are fed.
> Thank you, Lord, for daily bread.

As smart-aleck teenagers, we raced through with:

> Good bread. Good meat.
> Good God, let's eat.

My Episcopalian family tended to stick with the semistaid:

> Bless this food to our use and us to Thy service,
> And make us ever mindful of the needs of others.

I always thought that was especially nice since it included a sentiment of personal growth and good works.

Depending on who was chosen to say grace, we might also use the equally formal:

> Bless us, oh Lord, and these, Thy gifts,
> Which we are about to receive from Thy bounty
> Through Christ, our Lord.

Or Daddy's favorite:

> Come, Lord Jesus, our guest to be,
> And bless these gifts bestowed by Thee.

Other religions seemed to always ad lib—what a friend of mine called the "Jesus weejus" prayer:

> Jesus, we just gather here today ...
> Jesus, we just want to thank you for ...
> Jesus, we just want to ask you ...

You get the idea.

However it plays out, the act of saying grace traditionally and faithfully, no matter your religion, brings great focus to a family meal and connects everyone in a quiet moment of contemplation before the chaos of life continues around the table. There is great humility in the recognition of a higher power and the realization that the world is greater than what's outside our front door. And in a society so focused on getting and having, the very act of giving thanks reminds us that we should appreciate how fortunate we are and help those who are less so.

I knew people growing up who never said grace. It seemed very odd to me to sit down at the table and just start serving your plate. Rude, even. I also remember dinners on the church grounds, homecomings, and family reunions where the prayers would carry on so long I thought I might die of starvation before the blessing ever ended. In either case, whether it's so short you barely get your eyes closed or so long you wind up peeking to see who's sneaking a biscuit, grace always ends with a rousing "Amen!"

Unless you are Uncle Red.

Whenever the designated sayer of grace would finish in the traditional manner, Uncle Red would wink at me and continue on with:

> Amen! Brother Ben
> Shot a rooster. Killed a hen.
> Hen died.
> Ben cried.
> And all went home satisfied.

And only then it was time to eat.

And We Say Ma'am

"Yes, ma'am!"

I say it to this day as thoughtlessly as I breathe. As a child, whether I was speaking to my grandmothers, to my teachers, or to the house-keeper, I dared not leave the "ma'am" off the end of a yes, no, or thank-you. As an adult, I still say it. It's just what one does in polite southern society.

It was the way I was raised, the way my parents were raised, and the way their parents were raised. It is absolutely ingrained in my behavior. When I was growing up, heaven forbid I answered an adult's question with an uh-huh or uh-uh!

"We don't grunt our responses," Mama would say sternly. "What do you say?"

"Yes, ma'am!"

When Sonny was a little boy, I trained him to follow every yes, no, or thank-you that passed his lips with "ma'am" or "sir." Unfortunately, times have changed. As Sonny and I would go out and about, invariably some nice lady would ask my baby boy a question. "Do you like Spider Man?" "Are you in first grade?" "Would you like a sucker?"

Obediently he would respond, "Yes, ma'am!"

Adopting a tone of shock and horror, the woman would say, "Oh honey! I'm not *that* old! You don't have to call me ma'am!"

Oh, yes. Yes, he does, because that's the way I raised him. (And I'll thank you not to undermine me in front of my child.) The way some women carry on though, you'd think he had angelically smiled up at them and said, "Yes, you old biddy."

"Yes, you shriveled old crone."

"Yes, you ancient, crusty, dusty, so-far-past-your-dewy-prime-it's-not-even-funny old hag."

What they fail to understand is that being addressed as "ma'am" is not a matter of age. It is a matter of respect. It is a matter of deference to your elders, and by "elders" I mean anyone older than you. It is a matter of courtesy and manners.

I've seen scads of comments where women write how disrespectful and condescending they find it to be called "ma'am." Most of these women are not southern. Do they like being treated with disrespect? Being grunted at? Is being addressed politely just a nonissue? Has our society fallen into such a state of disrepair that common courtesy is shunned? Reviled?

Or maybe it's just that I'm old-fashioned. But if being polite and moving through society with civility and respect is old-fashioned, then so be it. I'm going to keep fighting the good fight one person, one interaction at a time.

Yes, ma'am, I am!

Standing on the Promises

Nowadays, when the workday nears an end and there's not enough time left to start another project but too much time to call it church and head to the house, we automatically turn to the computer to fill that void. We stare until our eyes burn at the glare of news, friend updates, celebrity gossip, sales. With aching heads and dulled minds, we creep toward the magic hour of freedom.

How did people fill the lull of the afternoon before computers and internet and smartphones?

Well, I'll tell you what my people did.

They played music.

At Mama's office, Malone Insurance & Real Estate Co. Inc., along about four o'clock in the afternoon when the last customer had gone, the mail had been taken to the post office, and the phone quit ringing, she and Barbara, her assistant, would pull out their instruments—Mama, the fiddle, and Barbara, the accordion—and commence to playing all the good old hymns that make you happy to be a child of God.

The brown, weathered hymnal they played from had dispatched a message of hope to generations of world-weary souls for whom the prospect of cities of gold far outweighed the prospect of another day hauling logs out of the woods and to the mill.

♫ I will meet you in the morning by the bright river side, when all sorrow has drifted away ... ♪

Barbara could play anything on the piano or the accordion, you only had to hum a few bars and her long fingers would fly over the keys and fill in your off-key gaps with all the right notes, plus a few embellishments to get you in the spirit.

> ♬ Precious memories, unseen angels, sent from some-where to my soul ... ♪

Mama, fiddle tucked under her chin and toe tapping time, would draw the bow over the strings, releasing the melodies she'd known by heart since childhood. Mama knows every word to every song ever written, no matter how obscure.

> ♬ As I travel through this pilgrim land, there is a friend who walks with me. Leads me safely through the sink-ing sand ... ♪

Sometimes Old Man Snookum Wally, a shade-tree mechanic from Okwaukee, would drop by with his guitar or fiddle to play a few songs with them. Once he brought me an old guitar he'd found at a flea market and showed me how to play a few chords. I still have the guitar although I never had any talent for music. I couldn't carry a tune in a bucket.

> ♬ I once was lost in sin, but Jesus took me in, and then a little light from heaven filled my soul ... ♪

Claude Platt lived about a block away. Every day, he'd drive over and park on the street in front of the office. First he'd go across the street to see what was happening at the police station, and then he'd come over to visit Mama and Barbara and catch up on the latest news, shadowed every step of the way by his big old redbone hound, Skafer. He didn't play an instrument, but he'd clap his gnarled, prize-fighter hands and chime in on the low parts.

♫ Love lifted me (even me), love lifted me (even me).
When nothing else could help, love lifted me … ♪

When five o'clock rolled around, the instruments went back into their cases, the lights were turned off, the door locked against the night. And we all headed to our homes, the lingering refrains of faith guiding our way.

Feeling the Cuteness

Today was a good day for no other reason than the fact that I was feeling the cuteness.

I mean really feeling it.

Now y'all don't think I'm having a narcissistic breakdown. In fact, to the innocent observer, I'm quite sure I looked the same as I do every day—like a forty-something working mama who manages to match her clothes and comb her hair nearly every day.

I have those days, probably more often than not, where my clothes don't quite fit right, my stomach is poochy, and I feel all out of sorts and just plain homely. There are the panty lines and what Granny called "eruptions" to contend with. Shine in the t-zone and circles under the eyes. At times like this, my attitude usually deflates as fast as my hairdo does, if not faster.

There is work, and band practice, and laundry, and things to sign, and checks to write, and dinner to cook, and dishes to wash, and scrapes to be bandaged, and bullies in school, and crazies on the road, and … and … and … at the end of the day you feel like a worn-out husk of a mama ready to take to your bed and let the chips fall where they may, even if it's out of the bag and onto the sheets.

But today was just different. I had a new outfit, and it not only fit well, it seemed to be remotely flattering. It hid what should be hidden, and it flattered what should be accentuated. The sweater I bought to match the outfit actually did match it. I had new boots. Enough said there. New boots!

If you have ever smothered yourself with Aquanet and permanent wave solution and fried your scalp with all manner of evil heated devices, you will appreciate this: my board-straight, baby-fine hair managed to defy all odds and not cling to my head like a dishwater-colored skullcap despite the fact it was a misty day. I even went outside, y'all! Twice!

But like I said, this really isn't so much about looking good as feeling good, and I felt good! I felt smart and sophisticated, clever and charming, worldly and vivacious. I felt like I could conquer the universe with my feminine wiles, disarming wit, and a pocketknife. I felt like a three-olive martini, straight up! And, by granny, I had me one.

You see, it's all about the cuteness. You can't buy the cuteness, although a new dress and boots help, to be sure. You can't create the cuteness. You can't borrow the cuteness from your best friend. You have to reach down into your very soul and feel the cuteness.

And if you feel the cuteness, really feel it, everyone else will feel it too. People will wonder how you manage to bring home the bacon and fry it up in the pan while looking so calm and rested. They will whisper hateful things behind your back about how you can possibly manage to host the bridge club, meet with the historical society, and still show up for PTO. They will question whether you visited the fountain of youth during AEA instead of Destin like you said. They will despise you, and you just won't care.

It's all in the cuteness.

And that, my dear sisters, is the secret to holding the world in the palm of your cute little hand.

A Firm Foundation

We are all familiar with the parable of the wise man who built his house upon the rock from the Gospel of Matthew. The rock in the story is, of course, the teachings of Jesus. But, ladies, I'm here to tell you that this principle applies to many things, chief among them fashion.

Just as the foolish man cannot build his house upon the sand, a fashionable woman cannot build her house of style on a squishy, bulging, dimply underpinning.

That's why the Lord gave us a firm foundation—foundation garments, that is!

Yes, I'm talking about girdles, longline brassieres, slips, and the like.

Did you ever wonder why Marilyn wasn't beset by panty lines or why Ms. Taylor didn't have a muffin top?

Foundation garments!

Were they comfortable? Well, no! But despite it all, these bombshells looked flawless.

Now, I will maintain until the day they press the toes of my pointy, red, high-heeled shoes down under the coffin lid that so-called "natural beauty" is as rare as hen's teeth. It takes work to look naturally beautiful because most normal folks, when presented in all their glory, just are not. Sorry, y'all.

And I, well, I know I'm not a dewy teenager anymore. But I also know that I can make the most of the foundation the Good Lord gave me, which is what recently drove me to the lingerie section of the store for just that—a foundation … garment.

You see, I have a sweater dress in my closet that has been taunting me. *Taunting* me, I say, because I am what you might call broad in the beam. Always have been. Always will be. No amount of squats, lunges, or other equally distasteful activity will ever change that. I'm good country stock.

So, thought I, "If you can't beat it, just mash it into compliance." And I set out to find the firmest foundation I could upon which to build my sweater dress house.

I came home with an Assets' convertible slip dress. It had it all. Smoothing. Shaping. Slimming. I was in business.

Come Monday, I got up and commenced getting ready for the day. I worked my way into my convertible slip dress (and I'm here to tell you, there was work involved) but I eased into my sweater dress. I too was flawless. Not a line. Not a bulge. Not a dimple.

Well, my sisters, the convertible slip dress is all fine and dandy when you spend the day sitting at your desk. I did notice on a few trips to the coffee pot and the copier that the convertible slip dress was wont to creeping up a tee-ninecy little bit, but not so much that a discrete tug wouldn't right it. And a little minor adjustment here and there is a small price to pay for looking sleek in a sweater dress.

It was not until I went to have lunch with my girlfriend that I noticed a slight issue with my convertible slip dress. While walking the block and a half from my parking place to the restaurant, I noticed more than just a tee-ninecy bit of creepage. My convertible slip dress was slowly but surely making its way north from my knees. The opportunity for a discreet tug did not present itself during the course of our lunch, and before I knew it, I was back out on the sidewalk making the trek back to my car.

With every step, my convertible slip dress was making a trek of its own … quickly. I was very hastily trying to make it to my car while taking teeny, tiny steps so as not to encourage the seemingly unstoppable creepage. I made it all the way to the middle of Twentieth Street, to the very center of the busiest lunchtime intersection in all of Birmingham, when—*fwoop*!

My convertible slip dress had made its way to the apex of my thunderous thighs and in a sudden and swift ascent rolled all the way up to my waist like a window shade gone wild, leaving me in the middle of the street with an enormous bulge of spandex where my previously hourglass waist had been.

One mad dash to the car later, the hem found and restored to knee length, I was once again flawless in my sweater dress and a little bit wiser. You see, it does you no good to have a firm foundation if it is not anchored securely to the ground!

Fur Is Dead! Long Live Fur!

One of the things I love the most about Alabama is that one day it can be nearly seventy degrees, and the next day snow showers are predicted. Yesterday I was very nearly glistening. Today I am shivering. Yesterday I wore a T-shirt. Today my first thought was, "Hot damn! I can wear my fur coat!"

Now before you go out hunting for your red paint and start screaming about fur being dead, let me go ahead and tell you that my fur coat is fake. There, I've said it—fake, mock, phony, pretend, artificial. But, boy, is it glamorous!

I have, however, been fascinated by fur coats as long as I can remember.

Mama has had several beautiful fur coats over the years. She had a champagne sheared muskrat coat and a beaver coat we bought on a trip to Montreal. It was on that trip to Montreal when I realized that coats were not confined to your everyday mink, foxes, rabbits, and other woodland creatures. It was there that I saw an orangutan coat. Monkey fur. It was weirdly orange and stringy. I had to put it out of my mind.

My favorite was a splendid chestnut-colored broadtail coat with a ranch mink collar that Mama had when I was a little girl. Daddy bought it for her at Raphael's, the swanky women's clothing store in Mobile, and I thought she looked like a movie star when she wore it! I remember resting my head on her lap in church and her covering me over with it. It was incredibly soft, and the mink tickled my nose. It was heavenly.

What was not so seraphic, however, were the beady little eyes that would invariably be staring at me from the pew in front of us. I was both fascinated and repulsed by stoles made from pelts joined mouth to tail around an old lady's throat. The glassy stare, the sharp claws, the little flat ears—all very menacing, if you ask me. And a little too close to the source for my taste.

Anyone who wears fur has to be able to mentally separate the fashion statement and its origins. If your coat has an expression, nay even a sneer, well, it just isn't quite as elegant.

But the stole, preferably headless, has secured its place as the answer to the southern lady's dilemma of wanting to wear fur while being constantly thwarted by unseasonably warm weather. Granny Mac had one with her initials stitched on the silvery satin lining, which is simply a *must* if you are going to wear fur. After all, when your mink is thrown casually over the back of the chair as you dance the night away at the Mardi Gras ball, how will everyone know it's yours without your monogram to give them a clue?

And they will also know where it was purchased. You see, when I got my first, and only, *real* fur coat for my eighteenth birthday, I was dismayed to find that the Metzger's tag had been sewn into the neck upside down! How could they? Didn't they notice? And, furthermore, even if every discerning eye at Metzger's had let this egregious mistake slip by, Granny would have surely noticed when she bought it. Wouldn't she?

Embarrassed to tell Granny that there was a flaw in her otherwise flawless gift, I turned to Mama. Could we get it fixed?

"Oh, no," Mama said with a laugh, "you don't want to fix it! It's supposed to be that way!"

You see, she enlightened me, when you are at that Mardi Gras ball and casually shrug your wrap off over the back of your chair, the label, upside down when worn, will appear right side up to passersby.

How deliciously sneaky, I thought.

And so it goes that I have always loved fur, its feel, the abject luxury of it as much as I've been fascinated by its societal nuances and its darker, snarling side. Thank goodness for cold snaps, synthetic fibers, and glamour without a sinister grin!

You Got to Recognize

I have a love-hate relationship with voice recognition technology.

I love that it is, in theory, an easy and convenient way to avoid having to use the keypad or talk to a human should you actually have the misfortune to reach one. I hate that while it recognizes that I do indeed have a voice, it does not recognize that my particular voice has a particular accent.

My first encounter with the technology that has since become my nemesis was at the Birmingham-Shuttlesworth International Airport. Brother was flying home from Rome (Italy, not Georgia), and his plane did not arrive at the appointed hour, nor was there an updated arrival time on the board. I marched over to the airline's desk to find out what was going on, but since it was the evening, the desk was unmanned and dark. There was, however, a sign taped to the desk with the 800 number for the airline.

So I pulled out my cell phone and called.

"Thank you for calling our airline," answered a nice robotic lady voice.

You are most welcome, I thought to myself.

The nice lady instructed me to speak the flight number about which I wished to inquire.

"4965," says I.

"I'm sorry. I didn't quite get that. Please repeat your flight number," says she.

I repeated, "4965."

"I'm sorry. I didn't quite get that. Please repeat your flight number," says she.

"*4965,*" I said a little slower and a little louder, because we all know that you are vastly more understandable if you just slow down and holler.

"I'm sorry. I didn't quite get that. Please repeat your flight number," says she.

"*4-9-6-5,*" I holler into the phone again, a little louder and a lot more emphatically.

"I'm sorry. I didn't ..." I hung up in frustration. And let me add that it is not at all satisfying to hang up on someone, even a robot lady, when you have no receiver to slam down.

As I was trying not to have a hissy fit right in the middle of the airport, it dawned on me. What I was saying was "4965," but what the robot lady was hearing was "foe-wer neye-un see-ux feye-uv."

Damn you, robot lady, and your emotionless pleasantries! Damn you, for not recognizing the southern accent!

From then on, I was all keypad all the time.

From time to time, I think that maybe I should pull a Don Williams and learn to talk like the man on the six o'clock news (if you don't get the reference, listen to him sing "Good Old Boys Like Me"). I mainly have this thought on weekday mornings a little after seven. "Why on particular days at a particular time?" you might ask.

The answer is number one in my heart and number one on my dial: public radio. Every morning I listen to my local station and hear the morning news delivered by a nice lady voice. She always says in a very soothing way, "It's 7:10. Thank you for listening to WBHM." Except what she really says is, "It's sehvehn tehn. Thank you for listening to double-ewe be aych ehm."

Every morning I look in the mirror and say, "Tehn. Ehm. Tehn. Ehm. Tehn. Ehm."

What I hear is, "Tay-un. Ay-um. Tay-un. Ay-um. Tay-un. Ay-um."

I just can't make my mouth say those two words. And I wouldn't sound like me if I did.

So at seven tee-uhn tomorrow, instead of "Tay-un. Ay-um. Tay-un. Ay-um. Tay-un. Ay-um," I plan to say, "You are most welcome."

After all, it's our differences that make us who we are—unique and beautiful, intriguing and special. You just got to recognize it.

Note: When I was writing this piece, my beloved husband asked me if I had finished it. "I did," I answered. At which point he mimicked me with a loud "Ah *deeeeee-uuuuhhhddd*." Please note that he lives in a house of North Georgia hillbilly glass and should not be throwing dirt clods.

All Y'all Should Read This

The most notable characteristic of the southerner can be narrowed down to the use of one little word—*y'all*, the second person plural form of *you*. It's *you* and *all* run together. This sleight of tongue makes a little word that defines an entire culture because no matter where in the world you go, the minute you let fly with a "Hey y'all!" everyone knows you're from the South.

Personally, I've always objected to being addressed as *you guys* because I am not a guy. I'm a gal, but no one says, *you gals*. My father-in-law does call me just plain *gal* quite frequently, which is endearing and sweet. But just as no one refers to me as *hey, buddy* or *hey, man*, so too should they not refer to me as part of *you guys*.

Down here we don't have to worry about offending good ole boys or good ole girls with improper forms of address. *Y'all* is gender-neutral. *Y'all* is all-inclusive. *Y'all* is friendly, familiar, homey. *Y'all* rolls off the tongue like a pat of butter on top of a hot biscuit.

Y'all can refer to part of a group ("Did y'all eat yet?") or, when added to *all*, a whole entire group ("Did all y'all eat yet?"). There is even the plural possessive *all y'all's* ("All y'all's dinner will get cold if you don't get to the table!").

The most important thing to remember, however, is that *y'all* is always, always, always plural. No one in real life ever walked up to one lone person and said, "Hey! Are y'all new 'round these here parts? What's y'all's name?" Are you listening, Hollywood moviemakers?

Y'*all* does not imply ignorance. Some of our most educated and influential brethren have retained this little nugget from our vernacular and use it every day, in all sorts of public forums, because it's just part of us. James Carville may smile and joke his way through serious political commentary, but make no mistake, y'all, he's no country bumpkin. Bill Clinton isn't either. And while Paula Deen may be dropping her r's, drawling, and yucking it up over a vat of gravy, she's built an empire on *y'all*, literally and figuratively.

One little word. One little contraction. The essence of a whole culture. Ain't that somethin', y'all?

A Brownie No More

Once a year every year, I am reminded of one of my greatest failures. My failure to become a Brownie.

It happens along about the time smart little girls dressed in sashes heavy with the badges of their accomplishment implore you to fund their pursuit of "courage, confidence, and character" through the purchase of sweet treats—Girl Scout cookies.

When I was about seven or eight years old, someone in my hometown decided to start a Brownie troop. We were to meet once a week at the Citronelle Baptist Assembly and learn how to be resourceful, clever, and creative young women. We also got to have cookies and Kool-Aid, *de rigueur* for any social gathering of the mid-'70s.

I went to the first few meetings, received a handbook, and raised my two little fingers heavenward while I fervently recited the Brownie Creed:

> On my honor, I will try:
> To serve God and my country,
> To help people at all times,
> And to live by the Girl Scout Law.

I was sincere. I was earnest in my study of the manual. I wanted desperately to become the responsible young girl in the illustrations—kind to animals and the elderly, able to create a tourniquet under duress, and adept at identifying indigenous trees by their bark.

I remember well the day of my downfall. The day I knew my hopes of sewing and fire-building badges would never come to fruition. The day I knew that I would never proudly wear the smart brown jumper and striped blouse with the Peter Pan collar. The day I knew I could never become a Brownie.

The end began with these words, "You girls will be excited to know that we are planning a campout on the banks of beautiful Lake Chautauqua."

A campout? Outside!? I was immediately filled with dread and horror.

Now many of you may think that because I come from the country, the far-flung recesses of Mobile County, Alabama, that I just love to sleep outdoors, on the ground, staring blissfully up into the heavens while the crickets chirp and the little froggies sing their songs. You would be wrong. It is precisely *because* I am from the country, the far-flung recesses of Mobile County, Alabama, that I do not, and will not, sleep outdoors, especially by a brackish, murky body of water.

As our apparently fearless, and obviously deranged, leader went on to explain how we would start fires and roast marshmallows and tell stories, all I could think of was the time when Baw and I were fishing at my cousin Sister's pond. We were sitting out on her little pier drowning some Catawba worms and having a ball. Sister's husband Jesse came down to join us. As the men stood on the bank and chatted, I continued to fish, dangling my little toes off the edge of the dock.

All of a sudden, Baw yanked me up by my overall straps and flung me up onto the grass while Jesse frantically began to beat at the water's edge with an oar. It was water moccasins, you see. A *nest* of water moccasins. Mere feet from where my little piggies had been.

Then there was the time when Baw and I were swimming at Puppy Creek. Tired of playing in the water, I was digging clay out of the bank to make little cups and saucers so that we could have a tea party. Baw was sitting in his harvest gold folding chair about thirty feet away watching me.

Now Baw always carried his pistol with him when we went to the creek. After all, you just never knew what sort of person might wander up. River people. I never really thought much about him carrying a gun until this day when I heard him say calmly and quietly in a tone, "Stand up slowly. Don't look behind you. And come to me. Now." I had never heard his tone before.

I looked over at him, and the gun was leveled in my direction. As I did like he told me, "*Pow!*" Baw fired and shot the head off a cottonmouth that had crept up right behind me.

As if this wasn't enough, I knew all about the rattlers, alligators, wild boars, bobcats, and black bears that shared our woods with us. Not to mention the less menacing but still disturbing armadillos, skunks, fire ants, and mosquitoes, all of which were guaranteed to be spending a warm summer night on the banks of bucolic Lake Chautauqua with a horde of little girls and their crumbs and noise and Kool-Aid. We'd be sitting ducks.

But not me. Not then. Not now. For you see, it was at that moment that I realized I was really only in it for the beanie, and beanies can be bought. Common sense cannot.

Come Swim in the Deep End

"Do you remember being the only little white girl who would swim in the public pool?"

Three times in as many months, I have been asked this question by as many hometown African American lady friends.

The answer? Honestly? No.

"Do you remember teaching the black kids how to swim?"

Sort of. I remember that if you couldn't swim, you couldn't play in the deep end. You couldn't play with me. I remember that I was lucky enough to get swimming lessons. I remember that everybody's mama and daddy couldn't afford to give them lessons every summer.

Here's what else I remember. I remember that I lived right across the street from the swimming pool—the catbird seat, if you will. I remember that it was a sparkling oasis of ice-cold, blue chlorination in an otherwise miserably hot, dry South Alabama town. I remember that I had a lot of friends, and we played Marco Polo, and raced, and did crazy dives off the diving board.

I remember that if my grandfather took me to the creek, there were no other children to play with. It was just me. And Baw. And the river.

Now that you mention it, though, most of those pool friends were, indeed, black. Now that you mention it, I do remember getting called nasty names, names that I will not repeat, because of who my friends were. Now that you mention it, I didn't care what those hateful people said then—and I don't care now. They weren't going to change me. They weren't going to stop me from playing with my friends. They weren't going to stop me from going to the pool.

I remember thinking how sad for them that they feel that way. How sad that they would deny themselves the fun of the public pool because of their prejudice. How sad that they would give up a whole afternoon of playing with some of the most fun people I knew just because of the color of their skin.

Back then, back in the early '70s, a few people felt compelled to say hateful, ugly things, but they had to approach me, look me in the eye, and speak their awful words out loud. They had to risk the possibility of a swift kick in the shins. Now, though, thanks to social media, people are able to spew their vitriol right out in public for all the world to see—a glowing screen separating them from the real world and the black and blue consequences. And spew they do. Freely. Recklessly. Thoughtlessly.

Freedom of speech is a right that we all have. It is a right I am thankful for, just as I am thankful for all of the freedoms we are granted by virtue of the fact that we are Americans. Freedoms that are unique to us, to the United States. Freedoms that many, many other people would give anything for. But just because you have this right doesn't mean you have to exercise it. As Granny used to say, sometimes it is better to be quiet and thought a fool than to open your mouth and prove it.

Nowadays, elections play out on Facebook, revealing enormous amounts of ignorance, selfishness, and hate. I have seen some of the most disgusting displays of prejudice—racial, gender, economic, sexual orientation—you name it. Forget about the least of these! Forget about loving thy neighbor as thyself! To hell with you, Samaritan!

Well, I wasn't raised that way. I was raised by a mother who took groceries to shut-ins no matter what side of the tracks they lived on. I was raised by a father who taught English at a historically black community college during the civil rights era. They instilled in me that you should help those who could not help themselves without question, without judgment. I was raised to stand up for what I thought was right and to defend those weaker than me. I was raised to treat everyone—old, young, black, white, rich, poor—with courtesy and with respect. I was raised at the pool.

Don't be alone at the river. Alone with hate, greed, and prejudice. Why don't you come to the pool and play in the deep end with me?

The Walk

One step is all it takes to begin a journey, whether it's a thousand miles or only one.

When I was a little girl, I walked a thousand miles through Citronelle. With no one to look after me, I stayed at Mama's office. More accurately, I strayed around Mama's office.

Left to my own devices for hours on end, I walked. I always left her office and went south on North Mobile Street. At the corner, I would wait for the revolving time and temperature sign on the bank to do a complete revolution so that I would be in the know.

Turning left onto State Street, I would walk a block past the First Presbyterian Church, which always seemed curiously locked up tight and in which I have never stepped foot to this very day. Come to think of it, First Presbyterian is probably the only church in Citronelle that I've never attended. But I digress.

On past the church at the next corner was Main Street, anchored on the south end by Newberry's Department Store. I would usually wander in to examine the new clothes and shoes and admire all the lacy embroidered handkerchiefs displayed in a long glass case near the front. It was air-conditioned in Newberry's.

Then on past the thrift store, which was always hot and dark and musty-smelling, past Mr. Carl's barbershop, where the men would all be gathered to talk, and past the Benson's flower shop, which always smelled of funeral.

On to Terrell's five-and-dime for a visit with Mr. Buster, the owner. Terrell's had everything from toys to costume jewelry to crochet thread to candy. Sometimes I would get a Sugar Daddy, or some wax lips, or candy cigarettes. You have to be careful with candy cigarettes, however, lest you be perceived as trashy.

Back out on the sidewalk, I would always stop to talk to Gladstone Trotter, who drove the cab. Gladstone ran his business from the only pay phone on Main Street, and if you needed a ride, you called that number. Rain or shine, summer or winter, Gladstone could be found leaning up against the storefront waiting for a call, usually surrounded by a few other fellows who would stop to chew the fat. I'm here to tell you that a little girl can learn a lot listening to what men say when they think she is not paying attention.

On northward to the Courtesy Food store. As shoppers moved in and out through the glass doors, great gusts of cold, cold air smelling faintly of onions and Pine-Sol would momentarily refresh me. A quick peek to see who was bagging groceries that day, then on my way.

Down through the alley by Andrew's Hardware, where I always cut through so as not to have to pass the liquor store to get back to Mobile Street. Lord only knows what kind of degenerates would be at the liquor store. I listened to the preaching. I knew. Best for a little girl to avoid it altogether.

Back on Mobile Street, I always checked for want ads in the post office in case I might recognize someone, and then I would meander next door to the Citronelle Rexall Drug to see if there was a new Richie Rich comic book. If I had a little money, I might get a vanilla Coke from the soda fountain. If not, I would smell all the perfumes while singing the Enjoli jingle.

Walking south on Mobile Street toward the prisoners washing the fire truck in front of the jail, I would arrive back at Mama's office, my journey complete—at least until the next day.

Although I didn't realize it at the time, every step in my ritualistic, block-wide odyssey was a lesson—lessons I still rely on every day. When to talk. When to listen. When to explore. When to be careful. Who can be trusted. Who can't. People are all different. People are all the same. Get by. Get along. Trust your instinct. Trust yourself.

All in the span of a block, walked.

The New Wild

He was bad.

Not wife-beating, bank-robbing bad, but rebellious bad. Wild bad.

He worked at the Courtesy Food Store and looked clean-cut enough in his short-sleeved white shirt and black tie. I'd see him when Mama did her shopping and sometimes when he was walking home along the railroad tracks.

But even though I was only a little girl, I still knew it. I could tell it. He was bad.

First of all, he had dark hair and dark eyes, a sure outward sign of inner badness. With all due respect to James Dean, you can't be bad with blond hair and blue eyes. Defiantly cute, maybe, but not bad. This fella had the blackest of black hair, a little too long, a little too shaggy, and eyes so dark they had no pupils.

I had also heard the whisperings. He was known to drink and maybe even fight. I wondered if he went to Old Glory, the local (and only) watering hole—and a place where people went to drink and maybe even fight.

But the legs proved my case beyond a shadow of a doubt. The legs were the final, undeniable mark of a bad boy. And not his legs. Hers.

Her legs, daintily crossed at the ankles. Her legs, long, long, long and ending in shoes with mile-high heels. Her legs, peeking out from the beneath the snow-white short sleeve of the Courtesy Foods shirt—*tattooed* on his bicep. Tattooed!

Had he been a Merchant Marine? In a motorcycle gang? Gone to Hawaii? Prison? Where else would one get such a thing!?

I couldn't help but stare. What did the rest of her look like? Reckon she was nekkid?

I couldn't tell! I couldn't see! That damnable sleeve!

And so began my fascination with tattoos.

Used to be seeing a tattoo was almost like a rare bird sighting. Next to nobody had one. You might see the occasional Hell's Angel in the gas station or an elderly veteran with a barely discernible greenish black mark on his forearm. But they were few and far between.

Now, everybody and their country brother has a tattoo or, better yet, tattoos. Skulls; flowers; devils; angels; aliens; hearts; koi, koi, and more koi; literary quotes; Chinese script (how do you *really* know that you have the symbol for happiness and not the symbol for slut); cartoon characters; portraits of loved ones; all manner of tribal design and emblem; family crests; Jesus; Our Lady of Guadalupe … it boggles the mind!

I'm incredibly intrigued by the artwork, the colors, the symbolism. I'm jealous of the talent it takes to paint a picture on someone's flesh. That takes guts, and I don't think I'd be brave enough to try. I admire those who do.

But the bad is gone. Getting inked is no longer rebellious. Tattoos are no longer hidden, taboo. In fact, it's nearly normal.

And, quite frankly, as much as I love to look at them, I don't think I really want a tattoo. I think I'll just keep on being rebellious in my own little ways. Hidden ways.

Unadorned is the new wild.

Fish Are Jumpin'

Ahhh ... summertime.

My summers were spent at the home of my maternal grandparents, Granny and Baw to me, under the watchful eye of Sarah, their house-keeper and my companion. Most of the morning, I would wander around their expansive yard, playing house under the scuppernong arbors, catching tadpoles in the goldfish pond, or picking blackberries with Sarah for a lunchtime cobbler.

In the afternoons, though, when Sarah had gone home for the day and Granny was busy with the Garden Club or playing bridge as nice ladies are wont to do, my Baw would take me on all sorts of glorious adventures. One of our favorites, fishing.

You may not realize it, but some of the best bait in the world is the Catawba worm—the fat, green, juicy larvae of the sphinx moth—and we just happened to have a Catawba tree in our pasture. No amount of plastic worms, fancy flies, or spinnerbait can compete with a wriggling Catawba worm dangling off a hook in tantalizing captivity. So up the ladder I would go with the cricket cage to pluck the unsuspecting critters from their host leaves. Sometimes when I'd squeeze one too much, it would excrete a dark, yellow liquid all over my little hands, and I'd nearly fall off the ladder screeching in delight and dismay if one were to "pee" on me.

Bait in hand, we would load up in Baw's old pickup truck, me sitting in his lap to "drive" us, and head out to wile away the afternoon with our Zebco rods and reels or, more often, just a cane pole. That evening, hot and sunburned, we would come home with our catch, usually a few nice bream or a catfish or two, to be cleaned and stowed away in the refrigerator for lunch the next day.

Nowadays, in the summer, as I sit in traffic trudging from meetings to music lessons to the grocery store listening to the sirens and horns and rap music, I long for the days of sitting by a pond with my Baw, listening to the quietude, sharing secrets and maybe a Peach Nehi, the endless days blending one into another like a hot and humid dream. Maybe tomorrow, I'll rise up singing … and dust off my Zebco.

Eat a Peach

"Baby, eat that peach over the sink! Don't get that juice on the floor!"

That's what Sarah would say to me in the summertime when the peaches were ripe and warm, their skins almost bursting with sweet, sticky juice. And she'd pull a chair over in front of the kitchen sink and stand me up on it. Then I could lean over, and eat the ripe fruit while the juice ran down my face and arms.

That's the way God intended us to eat peaches—with reckless abandon over a sink, juice running in rivulets down our chins, down our arms.

Granny had a huge farmhouse sink in her kitchen. The kind with the built-in drain board, cast iron with white enamel. There was a window over it.

The window looked out over a red brick patio with a big barbecue built on one side. Stone chimney. Rebar set in cement. Big enough for a whole goat. Gladiolus bloomed around the edges. A Lady Banks rose engulfed one corner.

Beyond the patio was a quince tree. And the clotheslines where the sheets would wave on the summer breeze. And a martin house. Beyond that was the horse pasture.

There was a shed where we raised biddies in an incubator. Where the tiller was. Where the spiders lived. By the shed was a scuppernong arbor.

All this could be seen from the window. All this could be seen by a little girl eating a peach over the kitchen sink. All this could be seen while the juice ran down my face and arms onto the white enamel.

Last Saturday, I smelled them before I even got close to the produce truck—peaches at the farmers market. Chilton County peaches. They were beautiful. Bright yellow bleeding into burgundy velvet. They were warm from the morning sun.

I bought a whole basket. You know I did.

As soon as I got home, I fished out a promising looking one—not too green, not too mushy—and stood over my kitchen sink to eat it, my stainless steel kitchen sink with a modern, gray glass backsplash. It doesn't have a built-in drain board. I don't have a window.

But as soon as I took the first bite of that peach, the very second the juice started tickling the underside of my arm on its way to my elbow, I was again looking at the red brick patio with the big barbecue built on one side. I could see the red and yellow gladiolus. The Lady Banks rose is blooming yellow in the corner. There's the quince tree, and the clothesline (Don't let the sheets touch the ground!), and the horses in the pasture. The martins are circling their house. Did we check on the biddies? I'm afraid of the spiders. Maybe I'll climb up on top of the arbor this afternoon.

Yes, that's the way God intended us to eat a peach.

Sook and Sarah

I stood at the foot of her grave, the Bahia grass tickling the back of my knees and a cacophony of summer insects loud in my ears. I hadn't come to Monroeville looking for her, but I'd found her.

Sook.

Twenty-seven years ago, almost to the sweltering June day, I stood at the foot of another grave. This one not yet marked. The red clay freshly turned. The Bahia grass. The bugs.

Sarah.

Sook was the elderly cousin of Truman Capote, who spent several years living with his kin in Monroe County, Alabama. While the other relatives worked, young Truman stayed at home with her and their dog, Queenie. "We were each other's best friend," he wrote—this young, lonely boy and this aging, eccentric woman.

Capote recounts their special relationship in *A Christmas Memory*. Mama recommended I read this autobiographical short story while I was researching an article I was writing. I wonder if Mama knew how much of little Audrey I would see in "Buddy," Capote's childhood nickname, how much of Sarah there was in Sook.

Sarah, charged with my care, as well as keeping Granny's house and cooking our meals, was my only companion while the rest of the family worked. Sarah. So tall, skinny as a rail, cheekbones sharp and high, hair braided in two perfect inverted french braids that circled her head. Sarah. Brown eyes filled, it seemed to me even at a young age, with sorrow.

Eyes that would sometimes light up with laughter as we played before going dark again.

As far back as I can remember, it was Sarah who dressed me, tamed my stick-straight mop into pigtails, or even braids like hers when I begged and her arthritic fingers would allow, fed me, read to me, and entertained me. We were each other's best friend—at least she was mine.

Our days were filled with bed-making, dusting, sweeping. Sarah let me "help." We would hang the laundry out on the line while we sang "Bringing in the Sheaves," which I thought was "bringing in the sheets" because that's what we did when they were finally sun dried.

> ♫ Bringing in the sheets, bringing in the sheets,
> We shall come rejoicing, bringing in the sheets,
> Bringing in the sheets, bringing in the sheets,
> We shall come rejoicing, bringing in the sheets. ♪

In the summer, we would pick blackberries in the ditch down by the road. Always looking out for snakes, we'd pluck the dark, black fruit, trying not to eat more than we saved but not always succeeding. When our bowl was full, we'd go back to the house and make cobbler, Sarah's long, brown hands covering my pudgy pink ones as we rolled out the dough for the crust.

Once I started school, I saw Sarah less, mainly during school breaks and summers. It was different then. I had friends my own age, playdates; I was old enough to go to the pool. I still helped in the kitchen, Sarah showing me how to fry chicken until it was perfectly "cripsy" and how to make chocolate icing in a double boiler, cooking it until it "looked right." She still reached out to tuck my hair behind my ear. She still hugged me tight.

I was in high school when Sarah got sick. She quit working for Granny. After more than thirty years with our family, after being there every day of my life, she was gone.

I went to visit her at her little house under the hill. It was dark and suffocatingly hot inside. Sarah was wrapped in a blanket. I kissed her cheek when I left. I knew it wouldn't be long.

Brother and I tried to slip into the back pew at her funeral, but Sarah's six children invited us to sit with them as we paid our respects. On the second row, I cried as if I was, indeed, one of her own. I had loved her like I was. I believe she felt the same.

Later that day, I stood at the foot of her grave. A grave not yet marked. The red clay freshly turned. The Bahia grass. The bugs.

Fast forward to Monroeville 2014. Husband and I decide to take a detour on the way back to Birmingham. We want to see the literary heart of Alabama. There is a walking tour pamphlet. See the Monroe County Courthouse; here's the Wee Diner where Gregory Peck ate; here's where Harper Lee's house once stood; next door is the foundation of the home where Truman Capote lived.

Wait. What?

The home where Truman Capote lived. The home where Sook lived. The home where they made all those fruitcakes, drank the leftover whiskey, made kites. The home of Christmas memories.

Continue on around Courthouse Square; notice the Monroe County Bank, site of A. C. Lee's office, and the *Monroe Journal*, which he also owned; here is the LaSalle Hotel, where Gregory Peck stayed; visit the cemetery where you will find the graves of A.C. Lee, Son Boleward, the inspiration for Boo Radley, and many of Truman Capote's relatives.

Truman Capote's relatives? Sook! I'd wondered if she was real. Now I knew she was. Not looked for, but found. As real as a friend can be. As real as Sarah.

And that's how I came to be standing at the foot of Nannie "Sook" Rumbley Faulk's grave, remembering my own best friend, tears mixing with sweat trickling down my face, the Bahia grass tickling my knees, a choir of summer insects singing them both home.

Why I Love Crime

I love crime. That is not to say that I enjoy it when acts of crime are perpetrated on the innocent. In fact, I hate and despise any and all acts of victimization, think it is bad, bad, bad, and believe that criminals should be thoroughly punished in a manner befitting their charge.

What I do mean to say, however, is that I am flat captivated by all manner of reality crime television. And tales of true crime. And criminal biographies. And crime scene photos. Mugshots. Fingerprints.

Why is it that I meditate so intensely on what caused the lawbreaker to launch down the slippery slope of malfeasance? Why do I imagine the culprit as a child and how, if raised under different circumstances, he or she might have turned out differently? For the love of Pete, where are their broken-hearted mamas? Why am I so drawn in by the sad, the lawless, the disenfranchised?

After some serious reflection, I have come to realize three things. First, I spent a good deal of my childhood at a police station. Second, while other little girls were playing Barbie, I was playing detective. And third, I have known more than one criminal in my life, and they were not all bad people.

I'll start at the beginning, when crime and criminals were right across the street and not hiding in the picture tube.

My grandfather and mother ran a small insurance agency opposite the police and fire station. When things were slow, Baw would walk over to catch up on all the goings-on. Of course, he always took me with him.

We went everywhere together, him always holding my little hand in his. Pete and Repeat people called us. Inseparable.

The front door of the police station opened into a small, dark waiting room. To the right was a little hallway through which you could see the cell door. Sometimes when I stole a glance toward it, some reprobate would be staring back through the little, high barred window in the gray steel door. It was scary but thrilling, like riding the swings at the Greater Gulf State Fair. Mostly, however, the cell was empty.

If I stood on one of the brown, vinyl waiting room chairs, I was tall enough to see the wanted posters with black and white pictures of devious criminals on the lam from certain and swift justice. Bank robbers, kidnappers, thieves, and murderers all with fingerprints, descriptions of their crimes, identifying scars and tattoos, and occasionally the warning "armed and dangerous." Their dead-eyed, menacing stares burning a hole right through you. Way yonder more interesting than Captain Kangaroo could ever hope to be.

Then there were the men of the Citronelle Police and Fire Department. Shiny badges, starched uniforms, guns. Jolly, joking, and smelling of Vitalis, cigarettes, and stale coffee. They would give me a Starlight mint or some confiscated brass knuckles, tell me a few tall tales of bravery and might, then send me to sit with Eva, the dispatcher, to wait for calls of grease fires, car accidents, or shootings that, thankfully, more often than not never came.

The men would smoke and talk of all the latest news about town, sometimes with loud, boisterous laughter, sometimes in hushed and somber tones. Who was caught with dope down at the river. Who was running around with whom. Whose kid was a troublemaker and just plain bad. Who had a few too many and got in a fight down at Old Glory. They whispered the secrets of a small town, and I got to hear them all. Of course, I never told. And never will.

Many of those men who protected our town have long since retired or died, Baw included, and there is a new police station, which I'm pretty sure has two cells now. But the stories told by these very real people about their friends, neighbors, and families, their crimes, their passions, and their foibles, sparked an interest that still burns to this day.

Why I Love Crime (the Redux)

A doll is boring. And vaguely scary with her fixed, blinking eyes. She just lies there. Staring.

A fingerprint. Now there is something flat interesting!

Here's what a doll has: hair plugs.

Here's what a fingerprint has: whorls.

Which sounds more interesting to you?

Baw had had the misfortune of contracting tuberculosis and spent many years recuperating from it and the surgeries recovery required. This process required long stints away from home and isolation from family and friends, both hard on a gregarious and affable man. To fill his time, Baw did many things. He drew. He wrote stories of his childhood. And he studied how to become an amateur detective.

He sent off for a fingerprinting kit that included dusting powder, some brushes, little white cards, and an instruction booklet, all packed in a neat little black case. He practiced around the house, dusting, transferring, studying, and comparing. Hours were spent peering through a magnifying glass at unique terrains of lines and ridges. He made notes on the little white cards of who was who, when the print had been taken, from what surface, and any distinguishing characteristics.

Little did we know that Baw would one day be able to put his skills to use to solve an actual crime.

I lived with my parents on a corner at the main intersection in Citronelle in the Lilly House, so named after the family who built it in the late 1800s. One day Mama came home after work to discover that the little black and white television that we kept in our kitchen was gone! Mama called the police and then called her daddy. When the men all arrived, an investigation of the house revealed that the only other thing missing was a pack of cigarettes and that there was no evidence of forced entry at any of the doors or windows.

As Baw and the detective walked around the house looking for where the thief had entered our home, Baw noticed that one of the old windows to the living room seemed to be up just ever so slightly. In a house as old as ours, the windows didn't lock anymore, but we never worried about it. We just kept them down—all the way down.

Out came Baw's fingerprinting kit. After a careful dusting, some teeny tiny little fingerprints appeared on the windowsill, prints too little for even a small man. The prints were, well, childlike.

The detective remembered taking a call that very morning from a man reporting that his fifteen-year-old son had stolen his car and was gone along with his two brothers, one of whom was only six years old. The boys and the car were nowhere to be found. The detective and Baw surmised that the two elder boys, who were known to be a little wild, had boosted their baby brother through the window to get the television and the cigarettes.

The detective put the word out that if the television appeared on his porch before the next morning, the boy would not be arrested and charged with driving without a license. Sure enough, when he got up the next day, the little television was sitting on his stoop, missing only the UHF antennae, which was never recovered.

Why I Love Crime
(the Final Installment)

My mama once said to me during one of our frequent political discussions, "I don't believe in the death penalty. I've known plenty of murderers, and they weren't all bad people."

Plenty of murderers, I wondered? *Plenty* as in "existing in ample quantity or number?" My sweet mama?

Well, yes. And, come to think of it, so have I.

I knew a man who, in the '40s and '50s, owned a honky-tonk just south of town and lived across the road from it. One night, a neighbor of his, fueled by a good deal of alcohol and in a rage over some unknown slight, proceeded to break all the windows out of the club building and then head across the road to see what the proprietor would do about it! Awakened by the sounds of banging on the door and glass breaking, the owner grabbed his shotgun, ran down the stairs, and shot the man he perceived to be a threat to his wife and young children.

Another friend of our family killed his father-in-law, who was notoriously ill-tempered and abusive. Again, alcohol was involved. A fight ensued, and only one man walked away.

One man had a wife who was known to run around on him. He loved her and tolerated her transgressions. But one night, out drinking with his buddies, they started talking about how she treated him and how he just took it. They teased and joked and put him down for not being a "real man." The next morning, he found his wife. And shot her dead. It was Mother's Day.

None of these three men were bad people. They were good people driven to defend their loved ones. Average Joes overcome by hurt and anger and pride. Family men caught up in bad situations. Not murderers, but people known to me who would go to the grave knowing that they had put someone early in theirs.

The Lilly House

It rained the day I was born.

And it has rained most every year on my birthday since then. That's what you get when you have a late September birthday. Rain. What else do you get? Spider lilies. The more rain, the more spider lilies.

As a child, I spent many an hour swinging by myself on the swing set in the yard of our big old rambling house. I would sing and swing, and sing and swing. Then I would pick flowers for a while. Then I would sing and swing some more. My favorite flowers were the spider lilies that would spring up every fall seemingly from nowhere. Not a bush, not a twig, not a bunch of leaves. Nothing to hint at the beauties to come. Just a green stalk shooting out of the ground crowned with a beautifully wild red frill.

I thought my house was named for the spider lilies that grew so abundantly because it was known as the Lilly House, but it was actually named for Leo and Millicent Lilly, who came to Citronelle, Alabama, in the mid-1880s. The Lillys established a dairy and raised chickens and sold eggs. By 1886, they had built the home that was ultimately ours—four rooms with a porch and a milk house on the back. The milk house later became our kitchen, and sometime along the way a bathroom was added too. Mrs. Lilly must have been an avid gardener because some ninety years later when we lived on that corner, there was still a field of narcissi, some asparagus that continued to come up behind the barn, and, of course, the spider lilies.

Japanese folklore says that if you encounter someone along the way whom you will never see again, spider lilies will bloom where you passed. Maybe that's why the spider lilies were so abundant at the Lilly House. With every autumn, with every birthday, with every song, with every swing, I was passing the little girl I was, and, from that moment on, would never be again, and slowly growing into the woman I am today.

A woman who still loves to swing and sing and pick spider lilies.

The Arbor

I have an arbor. I flat love it. My husband hates it—the bugs, the squashed and sticky scuppernongs, the smell of fermentation and rot.

I have an arbor because Granny had an arbor. And I flat loved it.

It was covered with muscadine vines growing down to the ground and high up into the trees. I would drag whatever lawn furniture and discarded household items I could scavenge or spirit away under the arbor's dark cover to create a playhouse, my own secret refuge hidden from the outside world. It was always shady and cool. Quiet, except for the hum of the bees and the occasional bark of a far-off dog.

I would mark off rooms with rows of pine straw and arrange old pots, pans, and broken plates in the kitchen. A rusty, metal chaise lounge from a long-forgotten patio set was my living room sofa. A bed of straw covered with an old horse blanket made a bed.

In my playhouse, I ate the muscadines growing at my fingertips and sand pears from a nearby tree, both sticky, sweet, late-summer treats. I watched birds nesting among the twisted branches. Sometimes I would get the ladder and climb on top, the old vines supporting my weight so I could lie down and watch the clouds blow overhead or feel the sun shining down on my face. I once entertained old Mr. No-shoulders, long, shiny and black, until he decided to carry on about his business.

That is why I have an arbor. I built it several years ago and planted three muscadine and three scuppernong vines. They have since grown to cover the wooden frame and drape down the sides like long curtains.

The vines have even ventured over into the fig tree, and in the spring, delicate, green tendrils seem to be reaching to touch the sky. In the late summer, the vines become heavy and droopy with fruit.

Sometimes, when Brother comes to visit, we go to the arbor and visit while we pick the muscadines and scuppernongs. As we talk, sometimes I will sneak one of the fruits into my mouth and pop the skin with my teeth, releasing the sweet nectar, and then spit the mucous-like center at Brother when he least expects it. I especially like it when I hit him on the neck or upside the head. It is one of my greatest joys as a big sister.

Mostly though, I find myself out under my arbor all by myself, lost in the task of picking the seemingly endless supply of grapes—only the low ones for me though; the high ones are left for the birds. I wonder why I haven't put a chair under my arbor where it is always shady and cool. I will next year, I always tell myself. I plot out rooms in my mind. I arrange imaginary furniture. I always keep an eye out just in case old Mr. No-shoulders decides to drop by.

Granted, I no longer have a need to play house. I can always go into my brick and mortar house where I have real rooms and air conditioning. But as the setting sun shines through the leaves, luminescent like stained glass windows, and I am serenaded by the buzzing of the bees and the occasional bark of a faraway dog, I am always loathe to leave my reverie.

I have an arbor. I flat love it.

The Essence of Lantana

My parents drank *film noir* cocktails—martinis (always gin, never vodka), sazeracs, B&B, scotch. When we were over the bay, there would be the occasional cold beer. Wine, however, only appeared on holidays, and champagne was reserved for wedding receptions, and then only those not held in the church hall.

When I moved to the city, I slowly became aware of wine and wine culture and that there was way yonder more to it than a stolen sip of Tickle Pink from an older friend. The regions, the grapes, the acidity, the soil! Who knew? I have to say that I am flat fascinated.

I am most enthralled by the jargon. I have the good fortune to be dear friends with the manager of a wine store, and if I perchance to drop by there in the afternoons, sometimes I get to take part in a "tasting." I get to hear people in the know discuss the intricacies of every little swallow in the most beautiful terms imaginable. They swirl, then sip, then spit, and then spill forth with such descriptors as "I get notes of saddle leather and orange essence," and "it is extremely fruit-forward, but the acidity makes me yearn for prosciutto and Roquefort."

"Oaky" seems to be bad. "Grassy" seems to be good.

I mostly try to be quiet, learn something, and not embarrass myself. I also smell and smell and smell and try to smell something other than ... well ... wine. Why can't I get a hint of blueberry and the worn pages of a Hemingway novel read by the sea on a stormy day?

One day, however, was revelatory!

I was again at the wine store trying to be quiet and not show my abject ignorance in a public venue. Again I was listening and marveling. Again I was smelling and swirling and smelling again.

Then it hit me like a brick to the head. Something familiar! An essence, a note, a hint of something humble, homey, and native. What is it? I can't quite suss it out! They may move on to the next bottle before I get to sound as if I too am in the know! It is ... it is ... it is ...

Lantana!

Before I could stop myself, I had blurted out "*Lantana!*" to the group of connoisseurs, who were now silent, staring at me with quizzical expressions, frozen midspit.

Do I get something Provencal like lavender? Something sophisticated like kid leather or rose water? No. I get lantana. The invasive, poisonous, leggy plant characteristic of every hardscrabble dirt patch where little else can eke out even the most meager life.

It is a plant, however, that was always featured in Granny's summer garden. Great mounds of orange, pink, and yellow that thrived in the dry south Alabama soil, that rose up to challenge the blazing sun. As a little girl, I made bouquets with it for my playhouse, breathing in its unique aroma. I thought its clusters of multicolored blooms beautiful and decorated my hair with its flowers.

Fortunately, the vintners did move quickly on to the next bottle, continuing their lofty discussions over a bucket of spit. But I could not move on from the aroma of that particular glass. It smelled like the summers of my childhood.

Lantana may not be very high-brow, but upon reflection and recovery from my embarrassment, I think it was an appropriate, albeit unconventional, descriptor. After all, lantana appears to be sweet and delicate, but in reality, it is strong, stalwart, and constant. Just like the wine. Just like Granny.

Manure and a Models Coat

This morning I realized that I have turned into my grandmother. I found myself in the backyard clad in my housecoat and sturdy moccasin slippers with my left elbow resting on my left knee while my right hand searched down through damp monkey grass for the base of an offending weed. This morning I pulled that weed and a handful more and cast them over the fence.

It all started with a cup of coffee with Husband on the deck, the morning unnaturally cool for August in Alabama. As we chatted, our attention turned to what we have come to refer to as "the backyard reclamation project." Our sloping, rocky backyard has become weedy and overgrown, and we have been vigilantly trying to fight back Mother Nature one little section at a time with mulch, gravel, pavers, and the carefully placed, hardy shrub.

We think we're winning, but it's a close one.

That's how I came to be in the yard, in my housecoat. There was a weed, audacious and mocking, peeking out in one of my carefully mani-cured flower beds. I could not sit still. A force greater than I could ignore compelled me to go down to the bed, stoop over, and pluck the offending interloper, and all of his insidious little friends, up by the very roots. Rear end in the air, head down, the realization hit me. I am Granny.

Now Granny was an avid horticulturist, and I, admittedly, have a black thumb when it comes to cultivating anything more than weeds. Granny would head out into the yard early every morning in her models coat and Baw's old loafer-looking man slippers. She and Leroy, her yard-man, would water, plant, haul, edge, mulch, and prune until the sun was high. Then, around eleven or so, Granny would head inside to clean up and get dressed for the day.

Every day, you would find Granny and Leroy, shoulder to shoulder, amongst the daylilies, camellias, zinnias, snapdragons, water lilies. The lantana, amaryllis, pansies, Johnny jump-ups, azaleas, iris. The roses, princess feathers, crinum, spider lilies, geraniums, impatiens. Granny in her housecoat, with a truckload of manure and a trowel, could grow anything.

And she won prizes!

Not only did she coax beautiful blooms from all manner of seed-lings, cuttings, and bulbs, she fashioned the blossoms into glorious ar-rangements. She entered every flower show the Citronelle Garden Club hosted and brought home ribbon after blue ribbon. She had a true talent for taking a dry block of green oasis and studding it with the best, hand-picked blooms from her yard until it was miraculously converted into a piece of living artwork.

But try as I might, with my garden clogs, Smith & Hawken garden kneeler, flowered gloves, and wide-brimmed sunhat, about the best I can do is not kill the hardiest of hardy plants. I overwater and underwater. I prune and transplant at all the wrong times. My Virginia creeper and poison ivy thrive, while my expensive store-bought plants shed leaves, turn brown, shrivel up, and die.

But maybe I've been going about it all wrong. Maybe today was a revelation of a different sort. Maybe it doesn't take expensive tools and gear to turn my backyard jungle into a lush Garden of Eden.

Maybe all it takes is a little daily attention, a truckload of manure, and a sweaty, dirty models coat.

Always Wear Good Shoes and Other Labor Day Advice

On Labor Day, I find my thoughts turning to Granny, one of the hardest-working people I ever knew. She gave me many pieces of valuable advice. For one, she told me to take business classes in college. As a teenage aspiring artist, I naturally rebelled against the idea but did it anyway and have been glad I did more times than I can count. She told me that you can get away with wearing cheap clothes, but you can't wear cheap shoes because your feet have to support you all your life. Again, as I stood behind a counter for ten hours a day, I realized she was right. Granny told me that one should never talk about money, politics, or religion when in the company of businessmen (or businesswomen, as the case may be). Time and time again, I have seen just how true this admonition was while witnessing deals made *and* lost based on issues that had nothing to do with the work.

Granny strongly objected to the term "redneck" being used to describe the stereotypical shiftless, slow-witted, fast-living, white trash natives of the South. Born in 1903 to a farmer and a schoolteacher and the oldest of four children, Granny knew what it was to work, to farm, to sew, to preserve, to build everything you needed to subsist. To her, the possession of a red neck signified back-breaking work performed bent over, neck exposed to the sun, necessary to further the well-being, if not the very survival, of one's family. The farmer, the mechanic, the shipbuilder, the roughneck, the logger—all rednecks, all respectable, honest laborers. For the indolent, however, she had no tolerance.

I remember Granny once telling me, in reference to her two sisters, "Eunice was the smart one, Lois was the beautiful one, but me … I just had to work hard all my life." And work she did, all the way up from teaching school when she was just sixteen years old to owning the bank in our town. And once she was in a position to, Granny supported others who wanted to work, whether it be through a loan from the bank or with her advice and counsel. All she expected in return was for the recipients to work as hard as she did, but the bar had been set sky-high. She was respected and respectful; she was smart but not condescending; she was stern but not hard-hearted, and she was years ahead of her time as a working woman in a male-dominated world, but always a perfect lady.

Unlike Granny, I had the benefit of a college education, a different era, and modern technology and conveniences. But thanks to Granny, I learned that being a woman is no excuse for not being successful; I learned to be brave enough to speak my mind; I learned that if you treat your counterparts, no matter what their station, with respect and dignity, they will return the favor; and I learned that an honest day's labor, whether it be digging a ditch, washing a dish, or running a company, is always honorable and to be commended.

The Power of Precipitation

She was almost ninety-nine when she died. Almost.

She attributed her longevity to rain. Not watching it. Getting wet in it.

I thought she would live forever. I think she did too, asking me once, "How old was Methuselah really?"

You see, Granny firmly believed that if you got wet in the first May rain, you would not be sick for the rest of the year. It seems to be true.

Granny did not diet; dessert was mandatory. Granny did not exercise although she worked in her yard daily. She did not take medicine, not an aspirin, not a spoonful of Creomulsion.

There was no tai chi, tae bo, kwan do, CrossFit, or karate. No zumba, yoga, troga, or Sweatin' with the Oldies. No treadmill, no recumbent, no elliptical. Certainly no running. Why run somewhere when you can get in your big, long Chrysler car and drive?

She didn't need it. For every year, as the fifth month began, we would perch at the ready waiting for a gray cloud to darken the blue South Alabama sky, listening for a distant rumble of thunder. Is the breeze picking up? Does it feel more humid?

Then as soon as the first drops began to fall, we would race outside and get wet in the first magical, mystical, healing May rain.

Now to be sure, Granny was no hard-bodied hottie. Not in her youth; not in her so-called golden years. If you subscribe to her notion of the power of precipitation, you must be well aware of the consequences and willing to accept them.

Your might see a slight jiggle when you lift your arm. (Gasp!) There might be a dimple or two in your thigh area. (Egads!) You might not have pecs. (Ladies, not really the most attractive look anyway.)

And you just might have to come to terms with looking just how you look, and being just fine with it. (Oh, the horror!)

Make no mistake. Granny prided herself on being well-dressed, neat, proper. But Granny didn't sweat a laugh line. She didn't paint her face all up, although a little powder and lipstick were *de rigueur*. She didn't dye her snowy hair, white since her late thirties.

And she did exercise. She exercised her mind. She read a great deal, but the *Mobile Press-Register* and the Bible she read every day. She was a cutthroat bridge player. Strategy. Subtlety. She worked crosswords and find-a-words. She conversed. She questioned. She believed.

So maybe the secret to longevity is not in a few drops of water from the sky, but in the contentment that comes with believing those drops will make everything all right—at least for one more year.

Either way, this year, as I do every year, when I hear the first distant clap of thunder, I will go stand outside and wait. Wait for the rain. Wait for contentment.

Thank you, Granny.

When Life Gives You Phlegm, Make Phlegmonade!

The cold and flu season is upon us—at least it's upon me in all its snotty, wheezing, hacking glory. As I snuffle about trying to think of something, *anything*, to make me feel better, I can't help but remember some of the home remedies Mama and Granny inflicted on me as a child.

Home remedies consist of one part tradition mixed with one part placebo, but little did I know as I gagged my way through many a "cure," that they were actually onto something.

Let's start with salt water nose drops.* When you're all stopped up and can't breathe, there's nothing like water up your nose to make you feel better! Actually, a gentle mist up the old schnoz helps irrigate those clogged-up nasal passages, flush out some of the goo, and keeps those mucous membranes moist. Not to mention that the salty taste in the back of your throat will remind you of last summer at the beach when that huge wave knocked you down, and you were sucked under by the surf and dragged through the sand until you managed to crawl up onto the beach panting and gasping and feeling like the whole Gulf of Mexico

---

*The information contained herein is intended solely as entertainment for the reader and is not intended as medical advice, to diagnose health problems, or for treatment purposes. It is not a substitute for medical care provided by a licensed and qualified health professional. Please consult your health-care provider for any advice on treatments and/or medications.

shot up your nose. But, hey. At least you were at the beach and not sick and shivering at home.

Along with the congestion usually comes a cough. You know what will help a hack? Honey. You know what helps it more? Garlic. Put them together and what have you got? The most vile cough remedy that will ever pass your lips. As a child, I dared not so much as clear my throat in front of Mama lest she come at me with a spoonful of her reeking remedy from a sugar-crusted Ball jar she kept in the kitchen cabinet. But "they say" that these supposed antifungal, antibacterial, antiviral, immune boosting superfoods do pack a powerful punch. That is if you can just choke a dose down.

Now Granny was a big fan of Mentholatum. It is an ointment. A salve. A petroleum jelly. A thick, greasy balm that when slathered on your nekkid chest and run by the fingerful up your nose is remarkably soothing and smells wonderfully of camphor and menthol. Now in my extensive minute(s) of research regarding the healing properties of Mentholatum, I have been unable to find any proof that it is in any way beneficial to someone suffering from congestion. In fact, I ran across several articles that intimated that it might not necessarily be good for you at all. Here's what I do know for absolute sure, when your granny slathers the salve on your chest, wraps a scarf around your neck to keep it all warm and gooey, and puts you to bed with a kiss, well, you just can't help but feel a little bit better.

Now if all of this fails to drive away the demons, there is always steam—the last, worst resort. Get a big mixing bowl and a bath towel. Then put a kettle of water on to boil. When it's good and scalding hot, pour that water in the bowl, hold your head over it *carefully*, and drape the towel over your head and the bowl, creating your own little sauna of healing. For a double whammy of medicinal mojo, put a dab of Mentholatum in the bowl before you add the hot water. Try to take deep breaths of the steam for as long as you can stand it. Yes, the snot will flow freely from your nose and into the bowl. Your eyes will burn. You will feel like your flesh is melting from your skull. But after just a little while, you will actually be able to breathe easier. Bonus: your complexion will appear remarkably clear and dewy.

As an adult, however, during those times when phlegm abounds, I choose to heal myself with what I like to call "phlegmonade," otherwise known as a hot toddy. This magical elixir combines honey with hot water, lemon juice, and the granddaddy of southern cure-alls, bourbon. You've got your superfood, your steam, your Vitamin C, and a little something to make it go down easy. You should be feeling better just reading about it! Now don't think that my toddy is just an excuse to drink during the day, a little nip for "medicinal purposes," wink, wink; nudge, nudge. There are some who say that because the alcohol dilates your blood vessels somewhat, your mucus membranes can better combat the infection. That bourbon is fighting for you. It's science, y'all. And who am I to argue with science?

Unlike a comforting warm beverage, the home remedies of my childhood seem to mainly work under the premise that what doesn't kill you makes you stronger. That is why I firmly believe an ounce of prevention is worth a pound of collards. Yes, collards. Whenever Sarah, who looked after me and kept house for Granny, would make collards, she would always give me a big cup of the potlikker. "Come here, baby, and drink this all up. It will make you strong," she would say. And she was right! As you cook those magic greens down, the iron and Vitamin C and all the other goodness leaches out of the leaves and into the broth, where it is usually (gasp!) thrown away! Don't let all those nutrients go down the drain; drink 'em up! Salty, smoky, warm, and vaguely greasy in a good way, potlikker was and still is one of my all-time favorite things. And I *am* strong. Just like Sarah said I would be.

At least I will be again. Soon. After one more toddy.

I Can Drink Gasoline

Leroy was Granny's yardman.

He was jolly, always quick with a joke or a funny rhyme. He believed that if you hung a dead snake over a tree limb, it would rain. He believed that garlic kept the haints away. He had biceps as big as tree trunks, or so it seemed to me, and he was the strongest person I knew.

So strong, in fact, that he could drink gasoline.

It's true! Every day Leroy brought his lunch and a big Ball jar of clear orange liquid that he kept in the garage refrigerator. Every so often he would take a break, get the jar out of the fridge, and tell Brother and me with a wink and a big toothless grin, "I'm so tough I can drink gasoline." With that, he would turn the jar up and guzzle it right on down.

We were slack-jawed in amazement. We had no doubt.

We knew that Leroy, or "Relolly" as Brother called him, had led an incredibly hard life. We had heard the stories. He'd been jailed for killing his father-in-law. He had injured one of his legs and now it was shorter than the other one, causing him to have to wear a heavy, platform shoe so that he could walk. We could see the callouses and scars, the clinched fist that would never open again. Another terrible injury.

But Leroy was always on top of the world. He would often tell me, "I've got it made in the shade down deep with a silver spade." He had no doubt.

Many years later, I found myself in the middle of a messy divorce, a single mother with a five-year-old who was depending on me. Betrayed, sad, scared, all I wanted to do was crawl into a hole and die. That is not, however, necessarily practical when one has a child to support and care for, so I muddled on.

One day around that same time I was sitting in my kitchen when an enormous "palmetto bug" decided to saunter across my kitchen floor. "Palmetto bug" sounds cute and beachy. It is not. In fact, this creepy brown intruder was the roach that broke the camel's back.

Normally, I would have screamed like a little girl for Daddy to come kill it. But there was no daddy. Or brother. Or husband. There was only me. And these were not normal times. I had had all I could stand.

I snatched off my flip-flop and smashed that palmetto bug into a greasy spot right where it stood with probably way yonder more force than was required. *So there!* I thought. *That'll teach you!*

High on adrenalin and fueled with vengeful thoughts, I scraped it off the linoleum, threw it in the garbage, and lugged the whole nasty mess up to the street. Good-bye and good riddance!

Walking back to the house, I thought to myself with a grin, *I'm so tough I can drink gasoline.*

Things got better after that. The dark year finally ended. A smart, sweet, funny college classmate found me, and I now call him Husband. Sonny has turned out to be a fine and talented young man of whom I am so very proud. I have everything in life a girl could ever dream of.

And now, when I walk up to my home, I think back on Leroy's other words. "I've got it made in the shade, down deep with a silver spade."

I have no doubt.

My Kingdom for a Dead Snake

Dawg Days are upon us. Go on, draw that syllable out just like the heat and humidity that threatens to stretch clear to Halloween. It's too hot to talk fast. Too hot to think fast. Too hot to do much besides indolently stand in the yard dribbling precious cool water on flowers as parched as you are.

This annual late summer conflagration, and the contemplation thereof, is some serious *and* Sirius business dating all the way back to ancient Rome when it was believed that the appearance of the Dog Star was a precursor to the hottest, most sultry days of summer. Back then, a brown dog would be sacrificed to appease the god in hopes that his wrath would be assuaged and the crops would not wither and die in the fields.

Now, I'd be hard-pressed to kill a dog no matter how hot it gets, but a snake is another matter entirely. According to Leroy, who helped Granny tend her vast gardens and hothouse and who was a veritable font of valuable information regarding all manner of superstition, all it takes to break the dark spell of Dawg Days is a snake. A dead one. Hung carefully over a tree branch.

Now I am unclear as to whether the species of snake matters, and there seems to be a debate about whether the snake should be hung belly up or belly down, in a tree or on a fence. But about one thing I am completely certain—this is some powerful mojo, and it works. Fast. Without fail. In fact, Leroy made it his common practice during the summer months to kill every snake he ran across and hang its carcass up in a tree. Consequently, we always had plenty of rain, but not too much, Granny's flower beds thrived to her delight, and two little towheaded kids thought he was a mystical rainmaker capable of performing miracles.

I warn you in advance, if you go hanging dead snakes in the far reaches of your yard—in the far reaches because you don't want company to come and there be a big, dead rattler right by the driveway scaring your guests, not because it works better if there is a distance—anyway, if you go hanging up dead snakes, forget where you put them, and go strolling about, you might be in for a nasty surprise. But should you decide you wish to pursue this line of defense against the most torrid, sweltering days of the year, you will be rewarded for your efforts.

Leroy guarantees it.

Oh, Fudge!

Granny was not a good cook. There, I've said it. She just wasn't. Granny had many talents, but they were all put into practice far, far away from the kitchen. Unless you count arranging flowers on the kitchen table, but that had nothing to do with food.

I remember one time when I was spending the night and Granny tried to make spaghetti for supper. Upon realizing that she was out of Ragu, she proceeded to pour a bottle of ketchup over the hot pasta. After all, tomato sauce is tomato sauce, right?

In theory, yes. In practice, no.

But there was one thing that Granny could make—fudge. And Granny didn't make any old cop-out fudge. She made the hard kind on the Hershey's Cocoa can. The kind that requires one to intuit things like "soft ball stage." The kind that, if you don't hold your mouth just right, well, it winds up being nothing more than grainy ice cream topping.

Granny could make it every time! She never failed.

And it was Granny's fudge that I looked forward to every Christmas. I would watch her slowly, constantly stirring, stirring, stirring the mixture. I would watch her let one drop slip off the end of the spoon into a glass of water. And I would watch her examine that drop to see if it sent the proper message of doneness.

If it was time, she would take the pot off the stove, add some butter and vanilla, and beat, beat, beat it with a wooden spoon until it started to look right. Into a buttered pan it would go, and a little while later it was a perfect square of fudge. Yum-yum.

I still make fudge every Christmas because it reminds me of Granny. Unlike Granny, though, I cannot make the Hershey's Cocoa recipe set up to save my life. I have problems with foods that must "set"—any sort of Jello dish usually defeats me.

I use the Carnation Classic Five-Minute Fudge recipe. It's a cop-out because it uses marshmallows and there are no ball stages or anything terribly complicated involved. I don't care. It always sets up, without fail.

Now just about every year it winds up that I only have one weekend with Sonny between Thanksgiving and Christmas because of a custody arrangement, bad luck, fate, and the alignment of the stars and planets. One piddlin' weekend for us to pack in all the fun holiday things we want to do. One weekend. Two days.

In past years, when he was younger, we'd go visit Santa Claus, we'd drive around and look at the Christmas light, and we might go see a Christmas movie if one was playing. But this year, now that he's a teen-ager, he didn't want to do any of those things. "Well, what *do* you want to do this year?" I asked him. "What is the one special Christmas thing that you'd really like to do?"

"Can we make fudge?" he asked.

So make fudge we did. Since we are products of too much Food Network, we started Saturday morning planning what flavors we would make, as if plain fudge isn't perfection. We dispensed with bacon (it's been overdone) and margarita (couldn't find lime flavoring), and we decided to try plain chocolate, chocolate jalapeño, peanut butter, dark chocolate cherry, white chocolate peppermint, chocolate chili, and s'more.

We made fudge all day long and into the evening. We made fudge until we were so tired and sticky we could hardly stand it. Some of the batches turned out great (you'd be surprised what a shot of Sriracha does to a recipe of fudge). Some not so great (apparently fudge flavored with maraschino cherry juice will never really set up, even if marshmallows are involved). And there were some that couldn't help but be good. (Did I mention plain is always the best?)

Sonny and I spent the day cooking and tasting. Measuring and stirring. Laughing and joking. We wound up covered in chocolate. We washed a mountain of dishes. We had to mop the floor. We ate fudge until we were nearly sick.

And we spent the day—our day—making so much more than just fudge.

Hershey's Cocoa Fudge

Ingredients:
- 3 cups sugar
- ⅔ cup HERSHEY'S Cocoa or HERSHEY'S SPECIAL DARK Cocoa
- ⅛ teaspoon salt
- 1½ cups milk
- ¼ cup (½ stick) butter
- 1 teaspoon vanilla extract

Directions:
1. Line 8- or 9-inch square pan with foil, extending foil over edges of pan. Butter foil.
2. Mix sugar, cocoa, and salt in heavy 4-quart saucepan and stir in milk. Cook over medium heat, stirring until you think your arm will fall off. When the mixture comes to full rolling boil, let it go without stirring, until mixture reaches 234°F on candy thermometer or, if you're like Granny and have a good sense of these things, until small amount of mixture dropped into very cold water forms a soft ball that flattens when removed from water. The bulb of the candy thermometer should not rest on bottom of saucepan.
3. Remove it all from the heat and add the butter and vanilla. *Do not stir.* Cool it all at room temperature until it's lukewarm.

Then beat, beat, beat it with wooden spoon until the fudge thickens and just begins to lose some of its gloss. Quickly spread into prepared pan and cool completely. Cut it all up into little squares and eat it up!

Note: For best results, do not double this recipe. This is one of Hershey's most requested recipes, but also one of the most difficult. The directions must be followed exactly. Beat too little, and the fudge is too soft. Beat too long, and it becomes hard and sugary.

Carnation Classic Five-Minute Fudge

Ingredients:
- 2 tablespoons butter or margarine
- ⅔ cup evaporated milk
- 1½ cups granulated sugar
- ¼ teaspoon salt
- 2 cups (4 ounces) miniature marshmallows
- 1½ cups (9 ounces) semisweet chocolate chips
- ½ cup chopped pecans or walnuts, optional
- 1 teaspoon vanilla extract

Directions:
1. Combine butter or margarine, evaporated milk, sugar, and salt in a medium, heavy-duty saucepan. Bring to a full rolling boil over medium heat, stirring the whole time until you think your arm will fall off. This method seems consistent no matter what recipe for fudge you use. Keep on stirring while it boils for four to five minutes. Remove from the heat.
2. Stir in marshmallows, chocolate chips, nuts, and vanilla. Beat, beat, beat it for one minute or until marshmallows are melted. Pour all that goodness into a foiled-lined 8-inch-square baking pan. Chill until firm, and then cut it all up into pretty little squares.

Beauty for a Day

There may come a time when you find yourself winding down a two-lane country road. And along that road you may see a field. And in that field you may see an odd grouping of bright flame-colored flowers.

Meet *Hemerocallis fulva*, otherwise known as the common orange daylily or roadside daylily. This tangerine titan of perennials is considered by some to be a weed, an invasive species. But weeds don't grow in perfectly straight lines. And weeds don't grow in the shape of corners.

You see, these daylilies mark the foundations where front porches once stood, where families lived, where generations were born and died. These rows are an attempt to bring beauty to a life that was probably not always beautiful and was more likely harder than the ground from which these blossoms erupt. The hardy nature of the daylily mirrors the hardy souls of country folk who would rather scratch out a living on their own ground rather than become beholden to another.

Granny loved the daylily and planted hundreds of different varieties around her home. Along with the common orange there were lilies with single, double, and spider petals, some with ruffles, some with "eyes." Lilies in every color of the rainbow from the palest peach to purples so dark they were very nearly black. Lilies bearing names like "Daring Deception," "Chicago Blackout," and "Emerald Dew."

There were daylilies that had been divided and traded for other varieties. Some were store-bought—ordered from catalogs and anxiously awaited. One was even a special hybrid cultivated by another local lily enthusiast as a gift to commemorate the birth of a granddaughter, me. We watched for buds to blossom, not wanting to miss a special showing that, twenty-four hours later, would become a soggy, wilted shadow of its former glory. We went out early to pick them for a special Sunday bouquet or to show off in the annual flower show.

Granny has been gone from us for many years now, but the lilies she cultivated so carefully continue to bloom with veracity, even in the face of South Alabama's sun and heat, hurricane and drought. I'm sure their myriad colors still bring joy to those who gaze upon them. And I know that their blossoms will ever greet the morning sun long after we have joined Granny beyond the clouds.

And one day her carefully cultivated flower beds will be reduced to random patches of flowers by the road. Although its name means "beauty for a day," there are countless years of history lost to books, lost to us, that are commemorated only by these lilies in fields. That is why this plain Jane perennial is no more a weed than the mighty oak. For even though its blooms may be fleeting, its rows will ever endure to mark a time in history that wood, stone, and mortar could not.

Love, Me

We were cleaning out her house. Packing up the dishes, the linens, the cutlery. The books, knickknacks, and bridge sets. Her mother's wedding dress and her daughter's baby dress. A forgotten shoebox filled with Borax and zinnias. Nearly a hundred years of living to be parceled out, stored away, or sold.

Her closet was emptied of its Alfred Dunner suits for church, house-dresses for every day, and models coats for lounging and pulling the occasional offending weed. Dress shoes and slippers all packed up for Goodwill. A final sweep of the floor, dust off the shelf, and this cheerless chore will be nearly done.

Reaching back into the far, dark corner of the shelf, she touched something. Something that had gone unnoticed during the cleanup. It was a little wooden box. It was locked.

Later that evening at home, she pried the lock open and lifted the lid. Letters. The box was full of letters. The letters were tied with a ribbon.

These letters told the story of young lovers who were always "old folks" to me. Teasing and flirtation. Spats and apologies. Endearment and devotion. Plans and dreams. Reality and survival.

Was it a tear that smeared the ink? Did she laugh at his pet names and silly jokes? A whole new story of my grandparents crowded my imagination and warmed my heart—the prequel to the white hair and bifocals I had always known. The ones I loved so much were now young strangers to me.

Together they endured the death of a baby child and a husband's grave illness. They raised a beautiful, intelligent daughter and sent her to college. They gained a handsome, bright son-in-law and saw two grandchildren born. They had their differences like all couples do, but they always had each other. Then, one day in November, she buried him.

But she still had the letters.

The love letter is a lost art. Lost to lives that are too busy (or too lazy) to take time to pick up a pen or go buy a stamp. Lost to technology. Lost to ways that are easier, but not better. Lost right along with beautiful language and heartfelt sentiment.

What will tell the story of your life? What will your children find? An email, text, or tweet? A CD or flash drive? A Facebook message with a little ♥ and an xxoo? Maybe ... if your past is not password protected.

Or will they find a yellowed envelope enclosing a faded letter, worn on the edges from rereading and smelling faintly of Midnight in Paris, inked with the inscriptions of adoration, devotion, and love. Just what will they find?

Talking with the Dead

I recently found myself alone in a car traveling a bleak and rainy back road with the ashes of a man whom I have never met. Alone for two hours.

"What did you do?" said my friend, as I relayed to her my somewhat odd circumstance.

"I talked to him," I answered, honestly.

I mean, what else are you going to do? It seemed impolite to do otherwise.

We (or, rather, I, since it seemed to be a decidedly one-sided conversation) discussed the inclement weather, his new home, and some general current events. I wondered if he already knew what was happening, but since he didn't interrupt me, I carried on. We (or I) sang along to the radio some as well. After all, two hours is a long time to keep up an amicable social discourse.

You would think my friend might be vaguely surprised that I had spent the better part of two hours chatting away with an urn of ashes, maybe even shocked. But she was actually only vaguely amused. She had, after all, implored her husband to dig up her beloved cat's carcass and move it across two states to their new home in Alabama. He obliged because he, like we all do, understands that southerners seem to have a unique relationship and fascination with their dead. It's almost as if they are not. Not *really*.

For instance, I called Mama shortly before Christmas to coordinate our holiday festivies. High on her list of things to do was getting fresh flowers to the cemetery to decorate the graves of her parents and Daddy's. And when I say high, I mean *high*, as in after shopping but before menu and wardrobe planning. After all, everyone needs some Christmas cheer, even if they are looking down on it from heaven. Or up, as the case may be, but we always hope down.

When I was a little girl, Mama, Granny, and I spent endless hours in old country cemeteries searching for the final resting places of distant relatives. They would recount generational relationships with such detail and accuracy that it made 1 Chronicles seem dubious in its recounting. We would also examine the graves of strangers and try to figure out who they must have been in relationship to their neighbors and what their lives must have been like. Lost children. War dead. Widows. All with real lives to be imagined and stories to be told.

Later on, after visits home from college, before I drove back, I would always stop by Pinecrest Cemetery to talk to Baw for a little while. Then I would drive over to Mount Nebo and say hey to Sarah, my childhood caregiver. I would brush away the debris and the occasional errant fire ant from their headstones, pull a weed or two, and be on my way assured that they were watching over me as a traveled. Who needs therapy when you can air out all your problems to a marble slab and invariably come around to a solution?

Southerners remember and recognize the birth dates and anniversaries of the dearly departed. We celebrate them, even if for a fleeting moment, as if they were still with us. In the case of those taken too soon, we imagine what they would be doing had they lived. For the elderly, we are thankful for the end of suffering, pain, and dementia and imagine their great reward found in a land of cloudless day.

We plan ahead for Decoration Day so that we can make our rounds to visit everyone. We surround ourselves with their belongings. Granny's wedding ring. Pawpaw's shotgun. A crocheted doily. A family Bible with notes scrawled in the margins. We remember our loved ones in the prime of their lives. Happy, healthy, carefree.

In the South, with its history of war and poverty, disaster and disease, death is just as sure as the fact that grits is always plural. We've learned to cope with and even embrace the inevitable with resignation, respect, and, often, humor. Is there really any other choice?

I had seen pictures of my traveling companion as a young man. Blond and tanned. Wearing his military uniform. Holding his baby daughter. It was this person with whom I talked during that long car trip from Georgia, not the inanimate jar of dusty remains strapped into the passenger seat. Had he lived, he would have been my father-in-law, and I wanted to make a good impression.

I know it may seem odd, but you know you do it too. It's really perfectly natural to talk to the dead. At least to a southerner.

Until they start talking back, that is.

Content in the Now

I remember filling out my application for the University of Montevallo when I was a senior in high school. Last name. First name. Middle name. Name you go by.

Hold the phone! "Name you go by?" Are they telling me I can pick any name I want to "go by?"

Now it didn't occur to me at the time that Daddy and his twin "went by" nicknames for their middle names. Or that I had a friend named Mary Louise who "went by" Sissy. I've always been unable see the Amazon rain forest for the twig, so I was captured by the enormous possibility in those four words—name you go by.

What could I "go by?"

Svetlana. Exotic, worldly, foreign. Maybe I could be a spy and smoke clove cigarettes and watch the frilly sorority girls from behind dark glasses with scornful disdain. Where is my beret?

No one knows me there. No one.

Maeve. The artist, barefoot, aloof, wildly talented. She drinks ouzo and dances around the fire with reckless abandon. Long skirts and paint-stained shirts.

I won't be the new girl—everyone will be new.

Missy. Fraternity little sister, dingbat with a heart of gold. Blonde and cute, studying interior design so she can share the healing powers of pink with all of mankind or at least Macy's.

Nope, can't pull that off.

Dixie. Beer drinkin', truck drivin', football watchin' gal who's one of the guys. She might spit, but it would be cute and not nasty. She can gut her own fish and look good doing it.

Nah.

I stared at that blank on the application. Thought and stared. Stared and thought.

Once I graduate and go off to college, I can "go by" anything I want! I can do anything I want. I can *be* anything I want. No longer the new girl. The redneck. The uncool. If I just set my mind to it and work hard, the world is mine on a silver platter.

Sort of.

Some people do graduate and go on to greatness realizing that expansive new chapter of bettering themselves and helping their downtrodden brother with the help of our Lord and Savior Jesus Christ, all while raising hydroponic strawberries, recycling, and rescuing abandoned puppies.

Unfortunately, and back in reality, that's not really how it works.

The rest of us start off with a head full of dreams only to realize that when you get there, no matter what you "go by," you're still the same person you ever were. Bad in math. Can't afford grad school. Country when country isn't cool.

We do, however, still manage to learn—both in the classroom and by being confronted by the real world for the first time ever. We try to better ourselves if by "better" you mean learning how to drink beer and not wind up in a pool of your own vomit. We make friends, some that last for a lifetime and some that don't last until the end of the semester. We quote Nietzsche and Led Zeppelin and marvel at our own intelligence and wit.

We learn to get by and get along. We learn that sometimes you fail, and it's not the end of the world. We learn that everyone doesn't like you, but many more people do. We learn that you can indeed eat Capt'n Crunch for three meals a day.

And we learn to *live*—passionately and ferociously—hoping for greatness but content in the now.

Subtle as an Ax to the Throat

I am a dreamer.

I am prone to drifting off into my own little world of ruminations, ideas, and plans. It seems to hit me all of a sudden like, and the world around me melts away into the roaring sound of my little wheels turning over thought after thought after thought. It is not uncommon for Husband to give me a little nudge and ask, "Where did you just go?"

Sometimes I tell him. Sometimes I don't.

Not only do I daydream, though, I sleep dream. A lot. Vividly.

I remember the first nightmare I ever had. I was around five years old. The Wicked Witch of the West was chasing me through the woods near Granny's house. I slip down on the trail slick with pine straw. I hear her evil laugh and look up to see the witch raising an ax above her head to chop mine clean off. I roll away, jump up, and keep running only to slip, hear the laugh, look up, and roll out of the way again just in the nick of time. Over and over, until ultimately I rolled away and right off the edge of the bed, waking up when I hit the hard wood floor. I didn't go into the woods without looking over my shoulder for years.

As a teenager, I had different dreams. Art school. A mall within an hour's drive. Neighbors. I dreamed of exchanging cutting witticisms with Dorothy Parker and the great minds of the Algonquin Round Table. I lived Saturday night seafood buffets at the Iron Skillet where I exchanged niceties with my fellow shrimp lovers. I dreamed of leaving the country far behind me and heading to Metropolis to live the glamorous city life.

I never made it to New York or even out of the state. I did make it to Birmingham, where going to the movies was not an all-day trip to town. Where you could buy a beer and drink it in public with your seafood buffet without your Sunday school teacher seeing you. Where there are neighbors, lots of them. Neighbors who walk by and wave. Neighbors with putting green lawns. Neighbors who set the apartment building on fire. Neighbors who fall out dead in the doorway. In their drawers. Hardly glamorous.

The other night, I dreamed I was at Mama and Daddy's house out in the woods. I looked out of my bedroom window, and where there had once been a thickly forested hollow was a treeless subdivision of little cheap houses with toothless, trashy people sitting in the doorways blankly staring out. I ran down the driveway wondering how I had missed this awful development. At the end of the driveway was a half-vacant strip mall. Across the road was another. I ran down the road past shack after dirt yard shack. I hollered at Mama that she should have just burned the woods down rather than sell out like that! What had happened to our little slice of Eden?

I ran until I woke myself up—heart beating, hot, and sweaty.

Now I daydream my way through busy days of work, school, sports, and band. Long lines at the grocery store, the bank, the tag office. Crowded restaurants and crowded malls. Hours spent in standstill traffic to go the whole nine miles from home to work and back again. But my dreams have changed.

Now I dream of getting back to the woods. I want to again think it odd to hear a car driving down the road after nine o'clock at night. I want to listen for the first whippoorwill. I want to smell the pines. I want to be free of neighbors. I want to be quiet. Rested.

Henry David Thoreau said, "I believe that there is a subtle magnetism in Nature, which, if we unconsciously yield to it, will direct us aright." I agree that there is a magnetism to the familiar, to the woods, to home. It is about as subtle, however, as an ax to the throat.

Murdering Killers Who
Might be Witches

When you live out in the country, isolated from neighbors, you take extra measures to keep your family and property safe, and my grandfather (Baw to me) was very vigilant. There was a gun behind every door, he had a pistol, and we had dogs that alerted us to any newcomer. As an added layer of protection, it was his habit to lock the door separating the bedrooms from the rest of the house once everyone had gone to bed. He performed this ritual every night, with a long, skeleton key and a lock that screeched and moaned in protest.

When Daddy was serving in the navy, Mama and I lived with Baw and Granny, her parents. We shared a bedroom at the back of the house where the other bedrooms were. Every night I would lie in my bed, waiting for the sound of Baw's footsteps coming down the hall to lock us in. He would roll back the hall rug, pull the door to, and coax the bolt into place.

Screeeee scraaaawww clunk.

We were safe.

But from what?

As a small child, I never gave the guns much thought. They were there. I was told not to touch them. I left them alone.

Periodically, unexpected headlights would creep up the driveway, and I'd see Baw get one of the guns and look out the front window.

Invariably, the headlights would ease back off into the darkness. Probably teenagers looking for love in all the wrong places and not realizing they were approaching someone's house. No threat there.

What did worry me was being locked into the back of the house. What was out there that was so bad, so scary, so threatening that we had to be locked away from it? The answer was quite obvious to my four-year-old self—murderers.

Killers.

Murdering killers who might also be witches.

I knew they were just on the other side of the door, waiting to burst through at any minute and kill us all to death. How did I know? I could hear their footsteps.

Every night.

I would lie in my bed, in the darkness, listening to Mama's breathing and the footsteps.

Tch. Tch. Tch. Tch. Tch.

Getting ever closer to the door. When would they get there? Why haven't they reached the door yet? Is one of them dragging a foot? Will tonight be the night, my last night?

Tch. Tch. Tch. Tch. Tch.

I would ultimately fall asleep, and wake up the next morning glad to have not been killed in my sleep and wondering where these murderous hordes spent the day. Behind the barn? In the tool shed? The woods?

When Daddy came home, we went back to living in our own house. There was no locked hall door. There were no murderers. No footsteps.

No more footsteps, that is until a few years ago.

I was home alone. It was dark and cold. As was my habit, I locked the house and then locked myself into my bedroom. After reading awhile, I turned out the light and rolled over on my side to go to sleep.

That's when I heard it.

Tch. Tch. Tch. Tch. Tch.

Footsteps!

Immediately I was four again. It had to be murderers!

Killers!

Murdering killers who might also be witches!

I waited for them to come. To burst through the door and kill me to death. *Who would find my body?* I wondered.

Then it dawned on me. I was the murdering killer who might also be a witch. For you see, the sound that I heard, that ominous tch, tch, tch, tch, tch was the sound of my own heart beating in my ear that was pressed into the pillow.

A flood of relief washed over me. I wasn't going to be killed to death—at least not on this night. And I laughed.

Laughed at my paranoia. Laughed at how irrational I had been. Laughed at the little girl with an overactive imagination. And laughed at the murdering killer who might also be a witch afraid of her own heartbeat.

The Bought Costume

When I was three or four, I got my first Halloween costume—a *bought* costume. Baw got it for me at Terrell's, the five and dime on Main Street. It was a happy witch, complete with black wig, plastic dress, and sparkly hat, not to mention the plastic mask, which was guaranteed to become damp with the condensation from your hot breath in under a minute. But who cared? It was a *bought* mask.

This is the only bought costume I recall ever having.

I waited anxiously for Halloween to finally come so that I could show off my fancy costume. I was so proud of it I wanted to wear it every single day. *It's the Great Pumpkin, Charlie Brown* signaled that the big day was nigh. It only came on television once a year, so you had be ready or resign yourself to waiting 364 days to see it again. I was ready.

Finally, finally, the long days passed, and Halloween came.

Mama helped me into the little plastic dress, arranged the fuzzy, black wig, and stretched the little rubber band around my head so that my mask was just so, and I could breathe and see, sort of. Mama put on her own witch hat and long black dress, and we were off.

We went out to town to trick-or-treat in the little residential grid of three streets that joined State Street to Lebaron Avenue. Back then, you were sure to get more homemade treats than not. Popcorn balls, cookies, possibly a piece of fruit or a dime. Every now and then you'd hit the jackpot and get a caramel apple. I still flat *love* a caramel apple.

Everybody would be out on their porches, neighbors chatting and trick-or-treaters running up and down the sidewalks shrieking and laughing. There were a few jack-o-lanterns smiling from the shadows, but not really much other decoration. Except for, that is, Mr. Stanley's house down on First Street. It was big and dark and spooky, and Mr. Stanley would lurk up on the porch in the dark waiting for some unsuspecting young'un to creep up his walkway, the lure of a sweet treat stronger than his fear of the dark. Then, when it was least expected, a ghost would fly down from the porch to greet the innocent. Mr. Stanley would laugh and laugh and then heap treats upon his little victim.

Down the street from Mr. Stanley lived the Carneys. They had a pet monkey that they kept chained to the porch. It wore diapers. This aberrance always struck me as way yonder creepier than Mr. Stanley because he was just scary one day a year. The Carneys and their screaming monkey were bizarre every day.

Back at home, I would sort out all my goodies and gobble up my favorites, at least those that I hadn't eaten during our trek through town. But while all the confections were naturally a delight, the real treat that year and every year after was the thrill of being out in our little community, walking up and down the streets in the cool, fall night air sharing in all the eerie fun with our friends and neighbors.

I still like to dress up like a happy witch, much to Sonny's dismay, but it always reminds me of that very first Halloween. If I only had a caramel apple.

Back to School

The first day of school. New clothes, binders, pencils, and paper. New hope for a better year, nice friends, and teachers that aren't too hard. A chance to reinvent yourself for the year. Find your niche. Make your mark. Change the world. The possibilities stretch out before you like the line in the cafeteria.

Even though I am no longer in school, I still get as excited about the first day as I did when I was four and started my educational pursuits at Mrs. Jones's kindergarten. Our school was a long, low cinder-block building behind Mrs. Jones's house on Lebaron Avenue. Every day started with the Pledge of Allegiance recited with our hands held over our hearts (I thought it was "with liberty and justice for Aud") and the National Anthem sung in earnest enthusiasm. We were young patriots during a seemingly never-ending, mysterious foreign conflict our parents called Vietnam. Thirty years later, my son would start his days the exact same way, war and all.

We spent most mornings sitting at round tables in groups of five or six. There were stories and singalongs and art projects. Then there was lunch, which everyone brought in little metal lunch boxes or paper sacks. A cheese, pickle and mayonnaise sandwich on light bread for me, thank you very much. No one cared if their sandwich wasn't in the shape of a star or if there was a peanut on the premises. We just ate whatever our mamas sent or traded for some delicacy a friend's mama had made like a bologna sandwich or a piece of cold fried chicken. We brought Kool-Aid in a thermos or drank from the water fountain.

After lunch we had a short nap on plastic mats that always seemed vaguely sandy, and then, it was playtime! Glorious freedom to run and scream and cut capers. There was a big swing set, a merry-go-round, and what was probably the most popular piece of playground equipment ever—a rusted-out junk car sitting on blocks. We swarmed its frame like ants, crawling under, over, and all around it. I remember climbing inside and sitting through the bottom of the enormous steering wheel while my friends rocked me from side to side.

Red rover; duck, duck, goose; crack the whip. We learned how to divide ourselves into teams, how to cope if you weren't picked, how to lead, how to follow, and how to win or lose graciously, for Mrs. Jones would have it no other way. We learned that, if chased, Frankie could run just as fast with crutches and a cast as he could without. We learned that if you pick up a snake and bring it into the classroom, the teachers would scream bloody murder, even if it is just a little one. I learned that if you kick the mean boy in the ankle just as hard as you can, he'll tell on you, and you will get paddled. Hard.

We learned so many lessons on that playground where there was no soft mat to cushion our falls, no hand sanitizer, and no time-out. So many more lessons than are found between the covers of a book. So many lessons that have made so many things possible.

Orange Juice

Orange juice.

Oh, how those two words haunted me.

Orange juice. Orange juice. Orange juice.

Sounds just like Audrey. At least according to Ronnie. Scrawny, freckled, buck-toothed Ronnie—my fourth-grade nemesis.

Once he made this brilliant connection, that's all he called me. Over and over again in his singsongy, squeaky voice. I hated the nickname. And I hated Ronnie.

All through the fall he doggedly continued to call me by his chosen moniker. In the classroom. At the buses. On the playground:

> Red rover, red rover,
> Send Orange Juice right over!

The worst part? You have to run right over. Everyone knows who Orange Juice is, so it's not like you can stay in the line quizzically looking around.

Who is this "Orange Juice" to whom they refer? Me? Certainly not.

I wanted to run right over and knock Ronnie's protruding front teeth down his throat, but all I could do was hurl myself through the clasped hands, tumbling past their grins. The faster I got back in line, the faster they would forget. Send somebody else on over.

I hoped that the long Christmas break would cloud Ronnie's

memory. Maybe distracted by toys and candy and Santa Claus, he would forget all about me. I was wrong. On the very first day back, even before the Pledge of Allegiance, I heard "Heeeeyyyy, Orrrr-aaaannngggeee Joooooossssss!"

I shot him my stoniest nine-year-old glare.

Wither, you moron; wither under my icy stare.

Ronnie didn't wither. In fact, my increasing exasperation only added to his delight. "Whatcha mad about, Orrrr-aaaannngggeee Joooooosssssss?"

January turned to February, and the class Valentine's Day party was coming up. We were going to have cupcakes and Kool-Aid. The teacher instructed us to bring Valentines to exchange. "Remember, bring one for everyone," Mrs. Turner said.

Everyone? Even my archenemy? Even ... him!?

The night before the party, I sat at the dining table with my box of paper Valentines. I looked at the cute cartoon kids with their cute cartoon animals. "Be mine!" "You're super!" "I'd be pleased as punch if you were my Valentine!" Mentally, I went down each row in the class addressing each little envelope. Pamela. Alice. Amanda. David. Darrell. Stanley. Rachel. Mark.

Ronnie.

Would he know if I spit in his envelope?

The next day, I got to school with my little sack of Valentines. The classroom was decorated with construction paper hearts, and the reading table held the cupcakes and Kool-Aid. Mama came to the school for the party along with some of the other mothers, and when everyone had assembled, Mrs. Turner said "All right, children, you may get up to trade your Valentines!"

We began to file around the room, putting a little card on every desk.

"Where's my Valentine, Orrrr-aaaannngggeee Joooooosssssss?"

Right here! I thought, and I reared back and kicked Ronnie as hard as I could square in the shin.

And here! And here! And here!

I kicked him until he crawled under the table of cupcakes to get away. I kicked him as the rest of the class stood in stunned silence. I kicked him for every time he had called me that awful name.

I kicked him until Mama dragged me away.

Mrs. Turner made me sit in the corner for the rest of the party. I didn't get a cupcake. I didn't get any Kool-Aid. I didn't care.

Happy Valentine's Day, Ronnie, I thought with a smile. *Love, Orange Juice.*

Mama Said, "Be Sweet"

"Be sweet now!"

"Y'all be sweet!"

"Love you! Be sweet!"

This is the admonition every southern girl hears from her mother as she leaves the house to go just about anywhere.

"Be sweet."

Why? Because despite their angelic looks and Miss Manners comportment, girls are not inherently sweet at all. And their mamas know that. They were, after all, once girls themselves.

Girls are, in fact, downright mean and hateful to one another. I know. I did three years of hard time at an all-girls school.

Be sweet, my ass I'd think under my breath as Mama dropped me off. *If I'm sweet, these vicious hussies will eat me for lunch.* And so it begins.

Too fat. Too skinny. Ugly. Knock-kneed. Pigeon-toed. So dumb. Too smart. Country. Hick. Wrong socks. Flat hair. Too slow. Too fast. Big bow. Little bow. Homemade lunch. Homemade clothes. Lesbo. Tramp.

You name it, and a girl can seize on it like a terrier on an old tube sock and make your life miserable because of it. Forget being sweet. Mama might as well have hollered, "Y'all survive now, ya hear!" as she dropped me off.

I'm sure being sweet does have a place in society, especially when it comes to the elderly, small children, and most animals. And I try to be sweet as a general rule. After all, Mama says I should be.

But it's hard.

Sometimes I don't feel sweet. Sometimes I want to just say something like, "For God's sake don't wear those pants again. You look like a mattress stuffed in a condom." But that's not very sweet.

Sometimes I want to say, "Why do you yammer on and on and on? I will drive an ice pick into my ear if you don't shut up." But that's not very sweet.

Sometime I want to say, "You drooling moron, how can you be so utterly stupid?" But that's not very sweet either.

Here's the thing of it. All these unsweet things? I sometimes want to say them to other girls (and boys too), but I mainly say them to myself. And that's really not very sweet.

Here's what Mama never did say: "Be sweet to yourself."

Easier said than done.

I have a sneaking suspicion that all the mean girls—and women—are mean for a reason. Bad hair day. Bad marriage. Bad life. Who knows? Here's what I do know. Whatever makes mean people mean really has nothing to do with you and everything to do with them.

I wish I'd known that when I was eleven.

We have to try to be sweet, though. If we can't be sweet to ourselves, how can we go out in the world as daughters, wives, mothers, and professionals and be sweet, or at least civil, to others? And if we are sweet, maybe it will be catching. Maybe that mean girl just needs somebody to tell her that all the horrible things she says to herself just aren't true.

Unless of course they are. But that has nothing to do with sweet and everything to do with reality. There's a difference.

Like I said, I try. I don't always succeed.

Things I Have Learned from My Mama

This is not going to be one of those Golden Rule-y, "My mother is a saint living here on earth" chapters. My mama is a woman of intellect and given to practicality and common sense. While she isn't an "all your dreams will come true" kind of person, she did pass along a few pearls of wisdom that I think about nearly every single day. Here they are:

If you can make a white sauce (*bechamel* to the hoity-toity), you can make anything. Cheese sauce, gravy, cream soups—all variations on the lowly white sauce. Master the basics, and you'll look like a gourmet.

Use eye cream every day and every night. Religiously. As if your life depended on it. You might be eighteen now and think you don't need it, but you would be wrong. Mama is, well, she's not eighteen anymore, but she's as beautiful as any woman half her age. Of course, a lot has to do with inner beauty, but eye cream has played a big part in the outer beauty.

Always have your own money. You might marry a rich man, but nothing says he has to share.

Sometimes you just have to buck up. Mama has always been very sympathetic to my whining and pouting and gnashing of teeth—to a point. I know, however, that I have exhausted her patience and made an utter fool of myself when she finally says, "You just need to buck up." She's right. I do. And it has always served me well.

There is no wrong time to eat ice cream.

Often it is better to just keep your mouth shut. These days we feel compelled to "express ourselves" and have "talks" *ad nauseum* about every little emotion, thought, or perceived injustice that flits through our vapid little minds. However, there are things that, once said, can never be unsaid. Don't say them. You will save yourself a lot of grief and drama. If you must say them or fall over dead, run out in the woods where no one can hear you and holler them out.

If you have a tummyache, it can be cured by lying down in a dark room with a pillow on your stomach. Or eat a bread pill.

Hens lay; people lie. (Refer to the paragraph above.) Proper grammar and usage is invaluable.

Listen more than you talk. You'll learn things.

Lipstick is essential.

Pay attention to the details. The devil is in them to be sure, but something worth doing is worth doing right.

There is a lot to be learned from the Psalms. Take the time to read them when you need to find a little extra grace or the courage to buck up.

Being a mother is not always easy or fun. But if you raise your children with the singular goal of molding them into the sort of adults you would like to have as companions—as friends—everything will turn out all right in the end.

Defiantly Straight

You've got to invoke a little southern Zen to endure the beautification process. Or drink. But we'll get to that.

Sixteen hours.

That's how long I was in my mother's home for a Thanksgiving visit before I found myself with not one but two different kinds of product in my hair.

My limp, straight, ornery hair has been a source of consternation to my mother my whole life, and one day, by God, she will conquer it and give me the bouncin' and behavin' blonde locks a self-respecting southern gal is supposed to have.

It started with my first permanent wave around the age of six. Mama managed to get one picture of me with a halo of golden curls. Then my hair went stick straight again. Defiantly straight.

For countless homecomings, holidays, proms, sweetheart dances, and cotillions, all the other girls would turn out with their hair jacked to Jesus. They had hair that exceeded the frames of our school pictures. Hair that refused to move in any amount of gale-force wind. Then there was me.

Over the years we have tried pin curls, pink sponge rollers, hot rollers, curling irons, back combing, teasing, rats (the kind for hair fixin' not for killin'), chemicals, a thing called a hot comb, the dreaded bonnet hair dryer, crimping, those spongy twisty sticks, sheer will, and a whole lot of Aqua Net to make my hair big. And it will get big, gloriously big ... for a little while. Then its stubborn straightness takes over making it point like an arrow to the ground.

An arrow bursting Mama's big hair bubble.

But my mother will not accept defeat. And this Thanksgiving I was on her turf. With the turkey in the oven, appliances of hair torture at the ready, and time on our hands, it was time to try again.

That's when the product came out. Applied only to the roots, mind you. Lifting the hair. You must lift the hair. *Lift it.*

Then came the heat. My right ear was nearly burnt slap off my head, but there is pain in beauty, y'all, and vicey versey. Deep, I know.

More heat. The pulling, tangling kind. The kind that feels like the devil is breathing his hot, sulfurous breath on the nape of your neck.

Then rollers. Lots of rollers. Unlike our hot rollers of yore, these Velcro thingies actually manage to grip my fine, wispy strands and bend them into submission. Plus they stick to your head so there's no need to gouge those pin things into your scalp to get them to stay. Progress.

Then I had to go let it set for a while. That's what the Macy's Thanksgiving Day Parade is for. And mimosas. You need something, for pity's sake, to make you forget how your ear stings and remember that you are just a hair away from real beauty—big hair beauty.

Not quite an hour later, giddy with anticipation, and certainly not with the aforementioned mimosa, we unrolled our way to the big reveal. Will it curl? Will it at least wave? Will all this time and effort and product and heat and Velcro be for naught?

Voila! Big hair for me. Well, sorta. Comparatively.

Now I know my hair will never rival Farrah's famed mane, but it was bigger than it normally is. Really. Downright puffy, I'd say. And it lasted. All day. Even in the South Alabama humidity.

Oh, sweet victory! Thank you, Mama.

Reflections on Being a Mama

For eighteen years I have been someone's mother.

I find that very hard to believe. I am someone's mama. The kisser of boo-boos. The holder of a little hand. The wiper of snot and other, much grosser things. Responsible for his formation into a productive member of society. Responsible for keeping him alive, clean, and fed—not necessarily in that order.

Me.

My mama always seemed to have it all together. She knew the answer to every question. She could sew. We never left the house without a hot breakfast. She owned a business. She found the time to read several books a week. She rarely lost her temper, and when she did, it was usually my fault.

I have not been that Mama. Here's what I have been. A single mother. A working mother. A mother who tried. A mother who made it up as she went along. A mother who did the best she could.

Just like, I suspect, every other mother out there—including my own.

So after eighteen years of trying to figure this thing out, I still don't have all the answers. Shoot, I don't have any answers. But I do have a few thoughts, so here are my reflections on this business called motherhood:

Be the mother your child needs you to be. Every child is different, and what works with one child, probably won't with another. Every situation is different. Every day is different. You know your child better than anyone, so don't let people tell you how to parent your kid. Do what you think is right for you and yours.

Talk to your child. Put the devices away. Talk, talk, and talk some more. And when you sit at a table, make your child a part of the conversation and expect him or her to contribute in a meaningful way. Don't prop some screen up in front of him. If they don't get used to being a part of the conversation when they are young, how in the world will they ever learn?

Read to your child. When your child wants you to read that same book for the umpteenth time, do it. And read another book after that. And pull that baby a little closer and read it to him again. Before you know it, he will be too old, and you'll wish you had. Oh, and they learn from being read to. Things like vocabulary, rhyming, and grammar. Important things.

Tell your child what he/she is doing right. We spend a lot of time telling our children what they are doing wrong. Spend just as much time—or more—telling them what they do well, what they excel at, what makes you proud, and what they do right. And while you're at it, use this same philosophy with your spouse, your friends, your coworkers. You'll see what a difference it makes.

Say yes. I bet I've said no a hundred, million, gazillion times. One day, I decided to say yes. You want to go out with your friends? Yes … when you finish your homework. You want some dessert? Yes … when you finish your broccoli. You want me to buy that thingamajig for you? Yes … when you do your chores. Now, I don't say yes to everything. I'm not crazy. But rewarding beats the pea-turkey out of punishing every day of the week.

Choices are bad. Little children don't need too many choices nor do they need to make decisions on their own. They don't need to be asked what they want to do, wear, eat, or watch. In their little minds, the choices are limitless. "What do you want to drink?" you ask in the nice restaurant. You know the choices are limited to what comes out of the Pepsi machine in the back. In the mind of a child, though, the answer can be anything from Bug Juice to puddle water and everything in between. That's why you wind up frustrated and mad, and they wind up in tears—overwhelming choices. That's why God gave them mamas—to make decisions.

Your child is not perfect. No one is. Don't put so much pressure on your baby to meet unrealistic goals, or your goals for him, or to be someone the child just can't be/won't be/isn't ever going to be. Appreciate him for who he really, truly is and what he has accomplished. Just because the child loses or fails at one thing—or many things—doesn't mean that he is a *loser*, or that you are a failure as a parent. It means that the child has learned a lesson and you have too, and that you can both go forward more informed.

Stay calm. If you can manage to stay calm in a stressful situation, things will usually turn out better. Calm is not my nature. Calm is something I have to work hard to achieve. Calm is sometimes (often, really) elusive. But if you can knuckle down and not fly off the handle, everyone will be better off.

Let your child be his own person. Blue hair. Mismatched socks. Quirky sense of humor. Whatever the phase is, just go with it. And if you don't like it but can manage to not make a big deal out of it, usually the phase will pass on by itself before too long.

Your child is not your friend. Sure, you can be friend-ly with your child. Have all the fun. Laugh all the laughs. Whisper secrets and dreams. But remember that you are still the mama. Children don't need to know everything. They don't need to be burdened with your drama. They don't need to feel like they have to take care of you. That's what your girlfriends are for. Children need to feel safe and loved and protected. They don't need a friend. They need a mama.

There you have it. Thoughts from an imperfect, still-learning, sometimes-eccentric mama who's managed to raise (and I'm certainly biased here) a pretty darn good boy in spite of herself. Oh, and there's one more thing I almost forgot.

You have to try really, really hard to mess up. And even when you do, by some miracle, that child will forgive you and love you anyway just because you are the mama.

Daddy's Little Girl

I am Daddy's little girl. The firstborn. The only daughter.

While everyone says I look like Mama, I am infinitely more like Daddy in temperament and personality. Daddy and I are *people* people. We like to talk to strangers. We like to joke. We have both been known to dance spontaneously if the right song comes on.

But what I am *not* is the bat-your-eyes-Daddy-buy-me-a-mink-and-a-Mercedes type of Daddy's little girl. Not hardly.

Daddy would not stand for that.

You see, Daddy didn't buy me everything I wanted. He instilled in me the value of hard work. From mowing the lawn (all gazillion acres of it with a push mower) to scrubbing toilets, no job was too menial, no task too common for his darling daughter. Daddy made sure I understood that everyone has to pitch in, no matter how laborious the task, no matter how dull, and no matter whether you just polished your nails because, as the poet John Donne would say, I was "a part of the main" and that requires pulling your own weight. As well it should have been.

And Daddy didn't let me slide through school on my good looks and charm. He made sure I learned. From the first books he read to me, trailing the sentences with his finger so I could follow along, through declining nouns and conjugating verbs on past algebra and chemistry until the day I graduated from college, Daddy always recognized my potential, even when I doubted it. Daddy made sure that I understood the value of an education, even when I was ready to quit. Daddy always encouraged me, even when I failed.

And Daddy didn't come to my rescue every time I tried to play damsel in distress. Daddy taught me how to change my own tires, how to balance my own checkbook, how to shoot a gun. I learned how to be self-sufficient, to rely on me and only me. I learned that some hurts are too big for Daddy to make better with a Band-Aid and some Mercurochrome, no matter how much he might want to. Daddy does, however, kill roaches and snakes, because that's what daddies do—just so you don't have to, even though you could.

And Daddy was adamant about manners. Good posture. Elbows off the table. No talking with your mouth full. Speak when spoken to. Be respectful. Why? Well, first and foremost so Brother and I didn't act like we were raised by wolves. But also because "good manners will open doors that the best education cannot." Clarence Thomas gets credit for the quote, but Daddy drove it home, every day.

If Daddy had cooperated with my grand life plan, by all accounts I should be driving the coastal highway through Orange Beach in a red Mercedes convertible, with perfectly manicured nails and coiffed locks, on my way to ride my thoroughbred onto a yacht while eating caviar from a silver spoon. But I am not, thank goodness.

I am far richer than that girl. I have been given gifts that will never lose their sparkle, will never wither and fade—invaluable, intangible gifts. That is why I proudly call myself *my* daddy's little girl.

The Intruder

There was an intruder in my bathroom this morning.

He was ugly and dark. He slipped up on me silently with evil in his beady little eyes. He made me go cold and hot all at once. He made my heart jump into my throat.

He was between me and the door. I was unarmed—not even a shoe, not even a book to heave at this fiendish prowler. He was advancing on me, backing me into a corner. I had no choice but to grab a can of hairspray, aim for the eyes, a leap like Baryshnikov over his writhing carcass and through the open door.

I was transformed into a little girl, running screaming down the hall. Only this time I wasn't hollering, "Daddy, come kill it," but "Husband, come kill it."

Which he did. Swiftly and violently. My hero.

Sweet Jesus, I hate a roach!

Why, I wonder, does this vile creature have such an effect on me? Why does it make my heart race? Why does my stomach churn at the mere mention of the *R* word.

It doesn't bite. It doesn't sting. It poses no real threat. It is small and easily disposed of. One stomp reduces it to a greasy spot. The rational, educated Audrey knows all these things to be true.

But the palpitating, shaking Audrey remembers that they fly. Sort of. A roach will launch himself into something resembling flight like a haphazard, rudderless bomber. You don't know where he will go. *He* doesn't know where he will go. But wherever it is, he will invariably land somewhere on my person, hairy legs and pointy feet clinging on for dear life as I swat and flail.

The terrified, wild-eyed Audrey remembers that roaches spread disease, and bacteria, and germs, and pestilence, not to mention ill will, fear, and intolerance. They are dirty and nasty. They look shiny and greasy. They might get something on me. Something sick and diseased. Something rare and catching. Will there be a cure? Will it be painful? Will it wash off?

And the hyperventilating, throat-closing Audrey knows there is no escaping them. No matter how clean you are, no matter how many little black motels you put out, no matter how often the nice bug lady sprays deadly poison in your home, if you live in the South, you will have roaches. It's a fact. Just like humidity. No escape.

For forty-odd years, I've tried to quell my unreasonable and visceral reactions to these horrible bugs. I've tried to resist the urge to blow holes in the floor with my .38. I've tried to breathe deeply and think that they are harmless little things—just a mutant watermelon seed ... with legs ... and wings ... and the capability of spreading infectious disease far and wide. Nothing to worry about. Really. Pashaw.

But every time one creeps up on me, all that rationale flies right out the window with me not far behind.

The Curse

(Dear readers, if you are squeamish or uncomfortable with a discussion of "lady time" and all things related, please rejoin me in a few pages. If you're not, well, here we go.)

Boardroom. Ballroom. Boudoir. High heels. Nail polish. Fancy dresses. Shiny baubles. Sparkling eyes. Girl power. Soul sister. Bring home the bacon. Fry it up in the pan. It's flat fabulous to be a woman.

Except when it's not.

Except when you fall victim to The cCurse. That's what they call it when you *become a woman*. You get "The Curse." Not fabulous. Not even close.

It starts ... *you start* ... when you're young—sometimes a teenager, often a preteen, and sometimes even as early as elementary school. Bye-bye childhood. So long carefree life. Years stretch out before you, measured in twenty-eight-day intervals and cotton pads. Years and years and years.

Decades.

There's no positive spin on "tThe cCurse." In polite company, most women don't even like to speak the words—period, menstruation. It all just sounds so ... so nasty. So clinical. So ominous. *You get your period.* A red dot of punctuation that is the end of all things, especially swimming parties, cramp-free days, and spotless sheets.

There's a reason no one refers to it as "the blessing," even when they're happy that *Aunt Flo has finally come for a visit.* A momentary sense of relief, maybe, then the cramps, the bloating, headaches, backache, and, of course, the obvious outpouring of "affection" from good old Aunt Flo.

But *you're a woman now*!

Joy. Can I take to my bed?

Hardly. One must carry on despite being *on the rag* (I can't even imagine how women managed before modern accoutrement!). Just because it's *lady time* doesn't mean you actually get any. Get up. Go to work. Feed the kids. Kiss the husband. Clean the house. Carpool. Bring a covered dish. Feed the dog. Empty the cat box. Groceries. Permission slip. Bills. Laundry.

Oh, and try not to bleed to death.

When you *become a woman*, a southern woman, you learn that it's a mortal sin to wear white after Labor Day … and for four to seven days of every month. No need to tempt fate. Bleach only helps so much. Black is your friend.

Because there will be blood. Sometimes a lot of blood. Every young girl learns quickly to seek out a friend who sits near you in class. When the bell rings, you whisper, "Check my skirt." You hold your breath. She gives you a reassuring "okay," mouthed silently, maybe a thumbs-up. Or she doesn't.

But you're prepared. You've learned to carry a sweater even if it's 110 degrees in the shade. A sweater looks fetching tied around one's waist in a jaunty manner. More fetching than a big red stain spreading across the back of your dress.

The mean girls giggle and point like it's not their worst nightmare. The sympathetic look away. You can feel your face getting red, redder than your skirt. Make an escape. Find the bathroom. Hide. Call Mama. Cry.

The next day you hold your head up like nothing ever happened.

Your *friend*, more like *frenemy*, is not a low-maintenance acquaintance. She requires *supplies*. Supplies that must be carried everywhere you go. *Lady things*. There's even a contraption called a *diva cup*. I can't even go there. It's just not *diva* to have to empty cups of blood. More like *scullery maid*.

You might have to tote around a supply of *sanitary napkins*. Note to the major corporations: It does not make *that time of the month* more bearable if it sounds like you have clean, starched table linens wadded up between your legs. I'm sure even Martha Stewart would agree.

These *supplies* must be bought at a store. In public. Where everyone who happens to glance into your buggy will see that you are *on the rag*. You make regular trips home from college so Mama can replenish your stock, saving you from the shame, the knowing look from the checkout lady, the inevitable run-in with the most dreamy boy. Ultimately, however, you'll find yourself forced to make your own *purchases*. You try to hide a neon green box of tampons underneath a sack of collards, behind a half case of beer.

I'd rather have people know I drink than know it's *my time*. That's saying a lot when you live in the Bible Belt.

What's on the other end of all this drama, you may ask. *The Change*. Hot flashes. Night sweats. Mood swings. Irritability. Weight gain. A one-way ticket to M-town. You might even grow a beard!

Even though being a woman isn't easy by any stretch of the imagination, I wouldn't trade it for the world. I walk in the shadow of a long line of strong, powerful women. Teachers, business-owners, farmers, wives, mothers—they forged ahead with grace, perseverance, love, kindness, and more than just a little grit. They did it all and had it all, not in spite of being women, but because they were women.

Curse? What curse? That ain't nothing but fabulous.

The Magnolia Tree and Its Gift

There is a cranny way back in the farthest corner of my brain. In that cranny lives a memory. Buried far beneath the births, deaths, tragedies, joys, holidays, and everydays that have piled on top of it, this little fragment has languished, long undisturbed.

At least, that is, until the other day when, *Ka-blap!* Just like that, it came rushing back all at once. A deluge of images. Like watching telephone poles race by the car window.

What, you may ask, drew this memory out from its peaceful, dark hidey-hole?

A magnolia—rather the scent of a magnolia.

It was about dusk. Husband and I decided to take a stroll through our neighborhood because that's what you do on a hot, summer night when you're too restless to stay inside but not motivated to do much of anything else. You walk. Slowly. Aimlessly. Feeling the still night air wrap you in its swampy embrace.

When the air is motionless and heavy, the summer scents seem enhanced, heightened, ponderous. And as we passed an ancient magnolia tree, the sweet, lemony tang of its perfume engulfed me and lifted me up to the tippiest of its tip-top branches, and suddenly I could see out over the piney woods of South Alabama. At least in my mind's eye.

You see, as a child, I was a climber. I'd climb any tree just to see if I could, and I had decided to climb Granny's magnolia tree. The one way down by the road. The one by the gate. The one I'd never conquered. A relatively low-hanging branch was all I needed. My arms reached for it. One great heave. Get a knee up! A leg! Push! Push!

And just like that I was on my way up.

Like a ladder, I climbed that old tree. Climbed until the branches were thin and the trunk swayed under my weight. Climbed until I couldn't climb any more. So I sat. I sat in the shade of its thick leaves, shiny and velvety. Sat among the blossoms. Sat breathing in the fragrance of its great, white blossoms. I sat for what seemed like a long, long time drinking in the sounds around me, the sights, the smells.

Looking toward Granny's house, I wondered if it was getting close to lunchtime. Had they called for me? Would I even be able to hear them? Would they hear *me* if I called out? Would they even miss me if I got stuck in that tree, never to be seen or heard from again, pecked apart by the buzzards that always seemed to circle?

The number one thing a tree-climber learns is that going up is easy. The trick is getting down. And now, for the first time, I wondered if I could.

With hands slick from sweat and grimy from the bark, I slowly made my descent. Don't look down. Just feel your way. Don't panic. One foot. One hand. There's a good branch. There's another. Hold on. Breathe. Just fill your lungs with the soothing scent of mother magnolia, and she will gently let you down to earth again.

And that she did, way back then, and the other night when a faint breeze blew the scent and the scene away.

Olfactory memory. That's what it's called when a mere smell triggers something deep within you.

A gift. That's what I call being transported back in time forty years straight to the top of a tree.

Long Live the King!

I come from a land where the peach is queen. There are peach parks, peach festivals, a real live peach queen, and even a water tower devoted to her luscious, ruddy being. For several months in the summer, every magazine, cooking show, and commentary is devoted to recipes for peach cobblers and peach ice creams. We are regaled with tales of eating peaches over the sink, while the juices run down your arms, and equally sappy, syrupy nostalgia for our southern sovereign and the barefoot days of old.

I, however, must profess my allegiance to another: the noble fig, the oft-ignored fruit of the gods, the redheaded stepchild of southern culture. In my world, the brown turkey fig is king.

As the proud owner of the mother of all fig trees, my anticipation begins when I see the first tiny green shoots of leaves heralding the end of winter and the coming of warmer days. With surprising alacrity, the tree leafs out, and soon little green droplets begin to appear. That is when time stops.

For months, I wait. And watch. Was there a slight color change? Are they bigger? Are they growing at all?

Then, one day, all of a sudden like, I see the telltale dark purplish brown peeking out from behind a leaf! Oh, frabjous day! Forget that floozy, the tawdry peach. The queen is dead; long live the king!

Silently, unheralded by the press and stars with spatulas and catchy phrases, in all of its dusky glory, the fig has arrived to share with me its succulent, honeyed goodness. I take what I can reach, eating them directly from the tree while the birds, bees, and wasps take the rest. I envision hot jars and pans of sugar syrup, a steamy kitchen boiling with candied delicacies.

Those old fuzzy peaches become but a distant memory. My summers will always be about the fig. At least until it's time for scuppernongs.

Uncommonly Good

I heard on the news that legislation has been introduced by several New England senators making it a felony to sell fraudulent maple syrup made from, as the reporter put it, "*common cane syrup.*"

Here's what I have to say about that—fine by me!

I think it should be a crime to taint perfectly good cane syrup with any sort of flavoring, including and especially maple! In fact, I think it should be a crime to disguise the nectar of this divine grass as anything other than what it is: a nearly perfect, multipurpose gift from the gods. *Common?* Hardly.

Sugarcane and I go way back. Baw planted a big field of sugarcane every year. He and I would go down to the garden to check its progress, and he would always cut me a piece of the stalk with his pocketknife and peel back the greenish purple peel so that I could chew all the sweet juice out of the fibrous interior. I would gnaw on it until it was practically desiccated for fear of missing even one drop of sugary goodness.

Little did I know at the time that this reedy confection from which I derived an *uncommon* amount of enjoyment could be used as fuel, both for people and machines. In India and Central and South America, various derivatives of sugarcane are food staples. Staples. Not condiments. Staples. Rum, a human fuel on a whole other level, is made by fermenting and distilling molasses. More intriguing to me, however, is the fact that Brazil and the United States lead the *world* in the industrial production of ethanol. The United States makes it from corn; Brazil makes it from … you guessed it … sugarcane! Yes sirree. The Brazilians are driving around in cars powered essentially by the same juice that fueled a rambunctious, towheaded little girl on a farm in South Alabama.

Now the juice of raw sugarcane has a particular, peculiar flavor that is incomparably good, but cook its juices down until they are exquisitely coffee-colored, vaguely burnt tasting, and viscous, and it's damn near perfection. In November, before the first frost, the sugarcane would be cut. Baw had it hauled over the state line into Mississippi to Mr. Brannon, who had all of the syrup-making equipment and the know-how. On the appointed day, early in the morning, we would ride over there to watch the magic happen. To begin with, the men would feed the cane through a big mill to extract the juice, which would then be strained to make sure there were no errant leaves, twigs, or yellow jackets to sully the final product.

If I was good and didn't get in the way, I would get a cup of pure, unadulterated cane juice to sip on. I could be *really* good when I wanted to. And, boy, if there was a whole cup of cane juice at stake, I wanted to.

Mr. Brannon had a long vat with divided compartments that sat over a hot fire of lightered wood. As the juice fed through the different chambers, it would slowly cook while Mr. Brannon walked up and down the length of the vat skimming, testing, watching until the transformation from liquid to syrup was complete. Waiting for it to get "right." Many hours later, when Mr. Brannon gave the signal, the men would leap into action putting the hot syrup into cans, and Baw and I, smelling like wood smoke and candy, would head home with our share.

Now I have had a lot of fancy desserts in my time, but not one of them holds a candle to my all-time favorite. Take careful note of this complicated recipe and maybe you can re-create it. Take a pat of soft butter and put it in the middle of a plate. Pour a few tablespoons of cane syrup on top of the butter in the middle of the plate. Mash it all up together with a fork. Get you a hot biscuit (homemade, not canned), cut it in two, and slather the butter/syrup concoction on the halves.

Then lap the whole gooey mess up with a reckless disregard for the sticky, buttery bits that drip back down onto the plate. After all, those can be sopped up with another biscuit. Afterward, be sure to lick the last tenacious crumbs from your fingers and marvel in how good and satisfying the whole experience was. *Uncommonly good.*

No offense to New Englanders, but just try to get that from a tree.

The Care and Feeding of Pickled Okra

I recently had the pleasure of traveling to New York City where, while shopping in a bookstore, I had the following exchange with the women at the register.

"So where's your accent from?" I am asked by one of the two nice ladies. I get that question a lot when I travel.

"Alabama," I say.

"Have you heard of pickled okra?" says the other lady, who was previously aloof but is now breathless and excited. "Every time I think of Alabama, I think of pickled okra. My mother got some as a gift. She put it in soup."

I must not have hidden my surprise very well, that look of *Excuse me. She did what with it?* because lady #1 said, "Well, what are you supposed to do with it?"

What indeed.

When I got home from the Big Apple, I was still troubled by the thought of putting pickled okra in soup. Raw okra, sure. Pickled? Blech! Where in the world did she get the idea to put pickled okra in soup?

So I did the only natural thing—I turned to Google.

I typed in, "What to do with pickled okra" and got tons of recipes to make pickled okra, but none that included it as an ingredient in a larger dish. "Uses for pickled okra" yielded the same result. "How to eat pickled okra" got me a message board, but little else new. No wonder the poor lady was so flummoxed by her gift from an Alabama friend.

So here's the skinny for anyone who has a jar of pickled okra and doesn't know what to do with it—eat it, y'all, just eat it! Eat it right out of the jar like a kosher dill, eat it alongside a tomato sandwich and let a little of the juice run over onto your potato chips; throw that limp old green bean away and swirl it all up in a Bloody Mary, fork some onto a salad, and smiggle it through some Ranch dressing.

But for the love of all that twangs and drawls, y'all, please, please, pretty please don't put pickled okra in your soup.

The Pearl Handle Pocketknife

The pearl handle pocketknife.

It was a gift from Granny to Baw one Christmas long ago. A gentleman's knife, it was a fine little thing, a knife you could take to church. No, it wasn't any ordinary, everyday knife to scrape the dirt from under your nails or sharpen a pencil. It was fancy, like a piece of jewelry you could carry in your pocket.

Somehow, though, in all the Christmas whirlwind of tissue, colored paper, and ribbon, the pearl handle pocketknife was lost. Baw was crestfallen. Despondent. A search was launched. Had it been thrown away with the trash? The knife was never to be found, and we never knew what happened to it.

And that's how the pearl handle pocketknife became part of family lore.

And that's why every Christmas since, when someone receives a tiny treasure, as soon as the teensy gift has been opened and exclaimed upon, someone will say, "Put it away! Don't let it be like *the pearl handle pocketknife!*" You can count on it. Every year.

This Christmas, the presents had all been opened, the pearl handle pocketknife invoked, and all the trash gathered and taken out to the Dumpster. As we were basking in the holiday glow and contemplating a preprandial libation, it occurred to me that I had not seen Mama open one of my gifts to her—her main gift—a string of quartz, pearl, and turquoise beads. Had I wrapped it? Where was it? Surely she had gotten it. Surely.

I tried to be sly.

"So, Mama, did you open all of your presents?"

"I think I did," she said.

"Did you have one from me? Maybe a smaller gift wrapped with a bigger one?"

"I got the socks you gave me," she said.

By this time, I had attracted the attention of Daddy, Husband, and Brother.

"Was there anything else in the sock bag?"

"Well, I don't know," she says. "The bag has been thrown away."

Thrown away? *Thrown away!* Just like the pearl handle pocketknife!

We dashed outside and into the alley where the Dumpsters stand. To our relief, our bags of trash were still close to the top. By perching on the retaining wall and leaning most of my upper body into the belly of the beast, I was able to reach our garbage bags and drag them out past the dinner remnants, commode parts, and other refuse. Frantically flinging wrapping paper right and left, and attracting more than one curious look from passersby, I managed to find the missing gift bag.

And the beads were still inside, waiting to be unwrapped. Waiting for Mama. Found, unlike the pearl handle pocketknife.

What else did we find among all that trash? A happy ending! So next year as we unwrap our gifts in a flurry of colored paper, ribbon, and tissue, instead of worrying about what may be lost forever, we can remember what was found, and laugh as we recount a new piece of family lore—the tale of how we fished a string of beads out of the Dumpster on Christmas Day.

Merry and Bright

Every year, as December approached, my paternal grandmother and her friends would start sharing large jars of friendship cake starter among each other. After all, what better way to show a little Christmas cheer and help a sister through the stressful holiday season than with a Ball jar filled with assorted canned fruits that had been fermenting for a month or more. Just perfect for the season of merriment—sweet, fruity ... and lousy with brandy.

Now I have always suspected that friendship cake (aptly named, I might add, because the more you eat, the friendlier you get) was really just a ruse so that nice southern ladies could have a little nip in the middle of the day. It wouldn't be seemly, you see, to knock back a preparty shot, no matter how many relatives were fixing to descend on you, no matter how many gifts were left to wrap, no matter how much cooking and dishwashing lay ahead. But a little fruit served over cake, or ice cream, or straight out of the jar, well, it's just a little dessert, after all. A sweet treat to give you a little sugar boost. And it would be positively rude not to partake of a gift. No matter if it is so stout that just removing the lid will make your pin curls droop. One mustn't be rude.

Come to think of it, many traditional southern Christmas desserts seem to include more than just a little of the sauce.

Mama always said William Faulkner was referring to Lane cake when he described a dessert that was "wicked as sin." Despite that characterization, Lane cake was always on our holiday menu. Created by

Clayton, Alabama, native Emma Rylander Lane, this layered white cake features a filling comprised of eggs, sugar, coconut, pecans, raisins, and, of course, bourbon. Now Emma must have been some sort of cooking phenom because making a Lane cake is no mean feat. There are egg whites to beat until your arm falls off, pecans to shell and chop, coconut to peel and grate. It's a flat lot of work. I can only imagine that after all that effort, Emma might have tasted the bourbon just to make sure that it would be the perfect complement to her confectionery creation. Just a teensy taste. Or two. Just to make sure the cake would be fit to eat.

Another Christmas favorite is rum balls. Crushed Nilla wafers mixed with Karo syrup, nuts, cocoa and a little 151 to hang it all together—does it get any better? There would always be a big plateful of rum balls at our family Christmas party. I remember sneaking them with my cousins as children. One bite and a warm feeling spread upward through my nasal cavities and down deep in my chest. Two bites and, well, I just felt warm and fuzzy all over. And what is Christmas really all about but feeling warm and fuzzy? Well, there is the birth of baby Jesus.

But sometimes it's all about fruitcake, at least in Prohibition-era Monroeville, Alabama. Truman Capote and his spinster cousin kicked off their winter holiday whenever Sook declared it to be "fruitcake weather." Off they would go with their savings from the past year to procure all the ingredients, including, and most importantly, a quart of bootleg whiskey from one Mr. Haha Jones, which he gave them for a promise of a cake. After days and days of work and after all of the cakes had been made and shipped away to their lucky recipients, Truman and Sook were left with just a little whiskey in the jar, just enough to divide in celebration of another year of fruitcake success. And celebrate they did with much singing and dancing in their otherwise somber, teetotalling household. "Road to ruination?" Hardly. Greasing the skids to unabashed revelry? Most certainly.

And that's what I like in a holiday—revelry. Merrymaking. Jollity. I like sharing recipes and traditions. I like noshing on a bourbon-soaked raisin or two and dancing with my mama in the kitchen just like Truman and Sook. I like the warm fuzzies on a chilly afternoon. And I love me some sweet, liquor-y desserts—the making, the baking, and especially the eating.

Now I'm sure that we had many holiday treats sans shinny.* Surely we did. I think. Maybe a piece of divinity or a sugar cookie or something. But one thing I am definitely sure of is this—our Christmases were always merry and bright. Very merry and bright indeed.

Friendship Fruit

Ingredients:
- 1 can pineapple chunks, drained
- 1 can sliced peaches, drained
- 1 can apricot halves, drained
  (or you can use three cans of fruit cocktail in a pinch)
- 1 jar maraschino cherries, drained
- 1¼ c. sugar
- 1¼ c. brandy

Directions:
1. Mix everything up in a two-quart nonmetallic bowl.
2. Put it to the side and leave it covered and at room temperature for three weeks, stirring twice a week.
3. Serve it over ice cream or pound cake, reserving one cup mixture for starter.

When you want to add to the batch, mix in one cup sugar and one of the fruits to the starter every one to three weeks, alternating fruit each time. If you can stand to, leave it alone and covered at room temperature

---

* Shinny is short for *shine*, which is short for *moonshine*. In *To Kill a Mockingbird*, Scout says, "Miss Maudie baked a Lane cake so loaded with shinny it made me tight." If you drink a lot of shinny, or even a little bit, you will certainly be tight, among other things.

for three more days before serving. You can also jar it up to give to your friends as presents! Be sure to add a little tag with instructions so they can keep their starter going.

Rum Balls

Ingredients:
- 60 Nilla wafers, finely crushed
- 1 cup powdered sugar
- 1 cup finely chopped pecans
- ½ cup melted butter
- 2 tbsp. light Karo syrup
- 2 tbsp. unsweetened cocoa powder
- ¼ cup rum (or bourbon), plus a little bit for yourself

Instructions:
1. Put everything in a big bowl and mix, mix, mix until it looks right.
2. Shape the dough into one-inch balls. I've found that if you dab a little water in your palms, the balls roll up better.
3. If you want to go the extra mile, you can then roll them in coconut or dust them with powdered sugar.
4. Put all your rummy little goodies in an airtight container with sheet of wax paper between each layer. Store at room temperature. These make great gifts too!

Happy New Year and Pass the Innards, Please

I'm about as southern as they come. And those of us reared below (*way* below) the Mason-Dixon Line are defined by many aspects of our culture, chief amongst them being our traditional foods. But one thing that I have never been able to stomach, literally or figuratively, is the idea of eating innards.

Yes, I said it. *Innards*. In-erdz, which are defined as "the internal parts of the body, entrails or viscera." Yum.

Now I understand that New Year's Day is a time to partake of the symbolic food item. I get that greens represent monetary good fortune. I will douse them in pepper sauce and lap them right on up. I will feast on the humble black-eyed pea, which is said to swell with prosperity as it is cooked. And I will more than likely indulge in a bit of bacon or some other sort of innocuous processed pork product so that I will forever move forward just as our porcine friends do as they root.

But I will not, *cannot*, ingest an innard. Tradition be damned.

I remember Granny and Baw were often known to ring in the New Year by enjoying a big steaming plate of brains and eggs for breakfast. *Brains*, y'all. Not bacon, not sausage—brains. The very idea is enough to put me off breakfast entirely. Scrambled eggs are just fine on their own, even runny ones. But mix them up with chunks of gray matter, and, well, there's just not enough ketchup in the world to disguise that.

And I must apologize to all you lovers of the chitterling, or "chitlin" as they are commonly called. I have smelled them cooking and cannot overcome it. I have eaten some truly foul-smelling cheeses that turned out to be just divine once you got them past the olfactory gland, but between my knowledge of this particular innard's function and its fragrant nature, I'll just have to say "no, thank you, ma'am."

Now Mama and Daddy will surely spend the first day of the year as they always do—indulging in head cheese or "souse." Now there are two words that I firmly believe should never, ever be used in conjunction. They are *meat* and *jelly*, which is just what souse is—a meat jelly. The long and short of it is this: you cook the creature's head until all the remaining meat bits give up the ghost and fall into the stock, which will then congeal due to the natural gelatins in the skull.

My parents will sprinkle some vinegar over this cold, pink gelatinous slab of meat goo (because *that* makes it better, she says as she rolls her eyes to the heavens) and gobble it up! Not me, brother.

Now I will confess to have eaten, when I was very young in the pre-chicken-nugget days, a pickled pig's foot or two, but that is more of an extremity than an innard. I have very nearly relished a vienna sausage perched atop a Saltine cracker, but that was on a fishing trip. And I really don't even mind the occasional smear of pâté, especially if I am in a foreign country. It is there, however, that I must draw the line.

If it looks like an innard and smells like an innard, then by Granny it must be an innard. And somehow I just can't get my arms up around the fact that eating innards will bring you anything more than a swift gag reflex, much less a whole year's worth of happiness, health, and prosperity.

Now can somebody please pass the cornbread?

To Dunk or to Crumble

Recently I read an article by John T. Edge, the venerable southern food writer and director of the Southern Foodways Alliance, in which he referenced his master's thesis written about the Potlikker and Cornpone Debate of 1931. Yes, you heard that right—the Potlikker and Cornpone Debate of 1931.

For nearly a month that year, the South, and a great deal of the rest of the nation, was held rapt by a back-and-forth debate between the editor of the Atlanta *Constitution*, Julian Harris, and Louisiana governor Huey Long over the merits of dunking one's cornpone into one's potlikker as opposed to crumbling one's cornpone into said potlikker. Would that I had been a fly on the screen door to follow a confabulation of such import! And make no mistake, it is important.

For the unfortunate among you who do not know, potlikker is the savory broth left after you cook up a mess of greens. As most everyone knows in these days of enlightened eating, when you cook those greens down, as we all like to do, many of the nutrients leach out into the cooking liquid. This brackish elixir is known for its curative powers, and to many it is the best part of the whole greens experience, especially when combined with a warm piece of cornbread. This marriage of absorbent bread and salty likker is near divine, but what is the best method to bring these two together on the plate? This question brings us to the debate of dunking versus crumbling.

If you crumble, you must carefully consider the cornbread to potlikker ratio—too little potlikker, and you've got a bowlful of broken-up, dry cornbread; too much, and you have mush. If you dunk your cornbread into the potlikker, you are left with a rapidly softening, crumbly piece of cornbread that you have to drag up to your mouth before the soggy end breaks off and falls back onto the plate. If there is breakage, then you are treading in crumbling waters, as far as I'm concerned.

I prefer neither method.

I like to take my wedge of cornbread (and I do prefer wedges from an iron skillet the way God intended cornbread to be instead of squares from a baking pan or, dare I say it, a muffin) and put it on a plate. Then I slice it cleanly, horizontally down the middle dividing it in half. Next I flip the top triangle over so that the points are facing away from one another and apply just the thinnest smear of butter to all of the exposed surfaces. Then, and only then, do I slowly, carefully spoon the potlikker over the cornbread, taking time to watch for maximum absorption and saturation of the potlikker into the cornbread with just enough running around on the plate for a little extra sopping, but not so much that it will make the cornbread fall apart into soggy bits.

There you have it. The potlikker gospel according to Audrey. When given the choice to dunk or crumble, I say *spoon*!

And for those of you who think, *Likker? Can't those rednecks spell?* it is most definitely *potlikker* and not *pot liquor*. This little matter was laid to rest by Georgia's Zell Miller in a letter to the *New York Times*:

> Dear Sir:
>
> I always thought The New York Times knew every-thing, but obviously your editor knows as little about spelling as he or she does about Appalachian cooking and soul food.
>
> Only a culinarily-illiterate damnyankee (one word) who can't tell the difference between beans and greens would call the liquid left in the pot after cooking greens "pot liquor" (two words) instead of "potlikker" (one

word) as yours did. And don't cite Webster as a defense because he didn't know any better either.

Sincerely,

ZELL MILLER

Lieutenant Governor State of Georgia

I bet Zell's a spooner too.

White Lily Cornbread

If you want to make good cornbread, it's best to use White Lily self-rising cornmeal mix and follow the recipe on the bag, although I throw in my own little twist.

Ingredients:
- Lard or Crisco
- 2 cups White Lily self-rising cornmeal mix
- 1¾ cups buttermilk or 1¾ cups milk
- 1 4 oz. cup of prepared unsweetened applesauce
- 1 large egg

Directions:
1. Preheat the oven to 425° F. Put a glop of lard or Crisco in your cast iron skillet, about a tablespoon or so, and put the skillet in the oven to preheat.
2. Combine cornmeal mix, buttermilk, applesauce, and egg and sugar. Mix well.
3. Take that hot, hot, hot skillet out of the oven and pour the batter into it.
4. Bake twenty to twenty-five minutes for ten-inch skillet or twenty-five to thirty minutes for eight-inch skillet. When it is just perfect and golden brown on the top, remove from the oven and serve.

MoonPie, MoonPie, Fly to Me

What is so good, so delectable, so prized that a seemingly sane person will jump a police barricade and run out in front of a moving vehicle to pluck it out of a horse-apple-tainted street and eat it?

A MoonPie, of course!

Originally intended to be a filling snack for miners, the MoonPie was first made in 1917 at the Chattanooga Bakery in Chattanooga, Tennessee. It is said that a bakery salesman was visiting a local company store and talked to a miner who complained that he often didn't get a lunch break. The hungry man wished he had a substantial snack to hold him over during the day.

"How big should it be?" the salesman asked.

The miner held up his fingers framing the moon and told the salesman that he wanted a snack just that size. The salesman went back to the factory, relayed the request, and so it was. Now, nearly a hundred years later, this iced, marshmallow-filled cookie sandwich has become a southern snack staple.

Originally the MoonPie came in three flavors: chocolate, vanilla, and banana. Now you can get them in strawberry, lemon, and orange as well as the ultratrendy salted caramel, but somehow these new flavors don't seem right to me. Too fruity. Too fancy. Vanilla is my favorite, followed closely by chocolate. I have never been able to wrap my mind or my mouth around artificial banana flavoring, but Husband prefers that one to all the rest.

The MoonPie is now the edible "throw" of choice for Mardi Gras revelers partly because it doesn't hurt much to get hit by one (unlike the Cracker Jack boxes they replaced) and partly because they are just dang good. Sometimes the revelers will throw you extras if you holler, "MoonPie, MoonPie, Fly to Me" as the floats go by. You can also ring in the New Year by watching a six-hundred-pound, electric MoonPie light up the night sky in Mobile, Alabama, which has the longest running Mardi Gras tradition in the United States. Need a new vacation destination? Try the MoonPie Festival in Bell Buckle, Tennessee.

How do you know if you are a true southerner? Aside from the requisite y'allin' and drawlin' and heart blessin', if you've ever eaten a MoonPie and washed its waxy, sticky goodness down with an ice-cold RC Cola, your card can never, ever be revoked. You're southern to the bone.

Fortunately for the MoonPie lovers among us, you don't have to wait for Mardi Gras or risk life and limb and possible arrest to get one. MoonPies can usually be found at the corner store, the Pig*, and any other similar purveyor of fine foods. And when you do get one, peel back the plastic wrapper to reveal this delicacy in all its round, gooey glory, inhale the sweet smell of this timeless treat, and thank your lucky stars (and moon) for that enterprising salesman and the hungry miner.

---

* "The Pig" is the colloquial name for the Piggly Wiggly grocery store chain.

A Glorious Mess

This morning I came into possession of something I can only term a "mess"—a glorious mess.

You see, Brother called me and said that he'd been given a gift, a downright *boon* if you ask me, but since he was going out of town, he'd be unable to partake in said gift and did I want it. My answer was an unequivocal you'dbetterbelieveitIamonmywayrightnowdon'tdoasingle-thinguntilIgetthere!!!

What was this benevolence? This act of kindness? This good fortune hidden in a garbage bag?

It was a mess of raw goober peas!

Just as fresh and purty as you want 'em to be. Brown, knobby, just smellin' like green. Why, they still had the stems on them!

Just how much is a "mess," you ask? Well, when this descriptive unit of measure automatically popped into my mind as I received this windfall, I wondered the same thing. I do know a bushel is a definite unit of dry measure, about eight gallons, and I know a bushel is made up of four pecks, there are two gallons in a peck, and so on into the high math of cups. But what about a "mess?"

I know you can have a mess of greens (and don't I wish I did!), which I think would be about an armload—as many as you can comfortably tote without a sack. But you can also have a mess of fish, which belies the dry measure concept. I think a mess of fish (again, I reiterate, don't I wish I had one!) would be about a full stringer, maybe a dozen or so.

Given these parameters and some general life experience, I would have to surmise that a mess is enough to feed your family and maybe have a little left over to share or put up for later.

Here's something I do know for sure. Those grand goobers are going to spend a few hours swimming in a boiling, briny bath this very night so that come Saturday, when all our kith and kin are coming to watch the football, we can gobble up this glorious mess, the juice running down our chins and our arms until we are absolutely sick with good fortune.

Hold the Sugar, Sugar

Let's get one thing straight: sugar has no place in grits. If you want to put sugar on your breakfast, eat oatmeal. Eat Cream of Wheat. Eat Ralston. But never, ever, under any circumstances, put sugar on your grits.

There. I've said it.

Grits are meant to be salty and buttery. Sprinkled with black pepper. Savory all the way. Add some cheese, maybe some sausage. Let some runny egg yolk ease up beside them. If some ham gravy trickles across your plate, it's all good.

But never sugar.

Shrimp and grits is good. Fried fish and grits is good. Grillades and grits is good. What's decidedly not good?

Sugar and grits.

Grits are ground corn, yellow or white. They are coarse. Polenta is not grits dressed up and visiting from Italy. Grits are grits.

And grits are never sweet.

Grits is singular even though it ends in *s*. You may have a singular bowl of grits, but you can't just have a grit just like you can't just have a spaghetti.

You don't put sugar on spaghetti either.

Grits are comfort food. Grits are breakfast, lunch, and/or dinner. You can slice up cold grits and fry the patties, preferably in bacon grease or butter.

Do not top these patties with sugar or, God forbid, syrup.

Grits will fortify you. Grits will stick to your ribs (and the pot if you don't watch out). Grits should be considered a health food. Why?

Because they are sugar-free!

Throw that box of instant grits away. I don't even want to know if your grits come in a paper envelope and the instructions include the word *microwave*. Take the time to make them from scratch, slowly. Savor the texture, the corn flavor. Get them good and salty. Drown them in butter. Enjoy them right down to the last forkful.

And remember, hold the sugar.

The Good, the Bad, and the Greasy

One of my favorite words is *greasy*. It must be pronounced gree´- zee, with long drawn out e's and a definite z. Not gree´- see. Say it with me: Greeee-zy.

Greasy comes up a lot in my life. During these last vestiges of a hot and humid summer, which has, as it often does in Alabama, faded into a hot and humid fall, every time I look in the mirror one word springs to mind—greasy. Forehead, nose, chin. All greasy. No amount of Cornsilk face powder can ensure a matte appearance. No amount of witch hazel can combat the shine. No dainty, paper facial blotter can absorb the oil. Alabama humidity will rear its shiny head in victory every time.

Face greasy is bad greasy. And there's more where that came from. A black smear on your starched, white blouse—bad greasy. Hair that looks like it's wet when it's not—bad greasy. Behavior that is more than a little shady—bad greasy. The orange solids circling the top of a can of tamales—bad greasy.

Then there is ugly greasy. Runoff from sprawling suburban parking lots into our local rivers and streams—ugly greasy. A rainbow of oil concealing tar balls below the surf that wash up on Alabama's white sand beaches, or any other shoreline for that matter—ugly greasy. If it coats the local flora and fauna in dark brown muck—even uglier greasy.

But greasy isn't all bad all the time. For instance, if your cast iron skillet is protected from rust with a layer of Crisco, that's good greasy. (According to the television commercial that featured Loretta Lynn,

Crisco will do you proud "ever time.") If your biscuit has a little butter oozing out the side and into a puddle of sorghum syrup—good greasy. If your fried egg is lacy and blindfolded from a hot bath in bacon drippings just like my Mama makes them—good, good greasy. That yumminess you lick off your fingers after a Sunday dinner of Mamaw's fried chicken—good greasy every day of the week.

Then there's poetic greasy. There is no other word that will appeal to a reader's intellect, emotion, and reason in quite the same way. While it is rare to find a verse that incorporates this weighty word, I remember fondly a poem from my childhood, one that we recited often, theatrically, with the dignity it demanded.

> Yo mama
> and yo daddy
> and yo great great greasy granny
> with the holes in her panties
> with a big behind
> like Frankenstein
> going beep beep beep
> down Sesame Street.

Take it greasy, y'all.

Guilty Pleasures

Rabbit is one of my guiltiest pleasures. Not rabbit*s*. Rabbit. On a plate, covered in gravy. Rabbit. It's better than squirrel, better than quail, better than gator.

Never mind the cute, floppy ears, soft fur, and big eyes. I can get past that every day of the week. In fact, I even had a pet rabbit as a child. The Easter Bunny brought me his little brown and white cousin one warm, spring Sunday morning. Baw and I made it a home in a hutch built in the chicken yard. We fed it, petted it, and tried to play with it. You should note here that rabbits don't much like being held, and, if they decide they are ready to be put down, will lay your arm open with the claws on their big old hind feet. Nevertheless, we took good care of it, and it lived high on the bunny hog.

One day, I went out to the chicken yard to visit our rabbit, but the hutch was empty! I ran to find Baw and tell him that our pet had escaped. But it was not a jailbreak. Baw told me very solemnly that the Lord had taken our little furry friend to bunny heaven and that he would be happy forevermore in paradise.

Of course I was as sad as sad could be, but who could argue that a rabbit wasn't better off hopping across heavenly meadows than he was in an earthly cage? Plus, that day Sarah made one of my favorite dishes for lunch—fricasseed "chicken"—and the world was right again.

Have You Got Game?

"Taste this and guess what it is!" Aunt Lois says to me one Thanksgiving morning while jabbing at me with a carving fork, a piece of grayish meat dangling from the tines.

"Go on; taste it!"

Now I don't know about you, but I want to be able to readily identify my food. Even at a young age, I didn't think I should have to guess what exactly it was that I was about to ingest. Plus, Aunt Lois had a history of cooking things that were, uh, a little too "organic" for my taste.

For instance, I was at her house one day near lunchtime and naturally the talk turned to what we should fix to eat. Unable to decide, we did what every self-respecting southerner might do when on the horns of such a dilemma—we went out to the garage to plunder through the deep freeze, that enormous coffin-like receptacle for all things blanched and frozen, fishy or gamey, or just plain too unwieldy for your normal Frigidaire.

Aunt Lois dug past the fish filets, the venison steaks, and even some frog legs and pulled out a freezer bag. "Let's eat this!" she said, holding up a bag with something, near glee in her eyes. Before me dangled two little carcasses pressed flat in the plastic, nekkid, arms and legs akimbo almost like they were shocked to death and flash frozen in their surprise.

"Squirrel!" She exclaimed, and off she went in search of the chicken fryer.

Squirrel. Oh my. Couldn't we just have a tomato sandwich?

Flash forward to Thanksgiving. Aunt Lois shows up at Mama's house with a huge roasting pan containing an unnaturally large roast smiggling around in some sort of *au jus* with a few onions and mushrooms. Once in the kitchen, she sets upon it with a vengeance, wildly hacking at it with a carving fork and a large blade akin to a machete.

"Taste it! Guess!"

I thought it better to guess *before* eating. Just in case. You never know with Aunt Lois.

Hmmm, I thought to myself, *what lives around here?*

Goat?

"No."

Wild hog?

"No."

Deer? *Please let it be deer. I'm running out of options.*

"No."

I'd seen what I thought was a bear track once. Lord, I hope not. Bear?

"No."

"It's *moose!*" she finally exclaimed. "A gift from a friend of mine who went hunting out West!"

Moose. Have mercy. No wonder it was so dang big!

For the record, if any of you, my dear readers, perchance to go out West and think to bring me a gift, I'd much prefer something that either makes me look good (like jewelry) or smell good (like perfume). I would just as soon not be remembered with a hunk of dead animal flesh, thank you very much.

But the same can't be said for Aunt Lois, once an ace hunter her own self. Aunt Lois, who has a room full of mounted heads from deer she felled. Aunt Lois, sweet, flirty, mischievous. Aunt Lois, who can gut a fish or a squirrel or a deer without ever so much as chipping her frosty pink nail polish. Aunt Lois, who doesn't take no for an answer.

So taste I did. Gray, dense, gamy, a little too chewy. *But if you slog it through some gravy, like most not-quite-palatable things, it wasn't half bad. In The Maine Woods*, Henry David Thoreau likened moose to "tender beef, with perhaps more flavour; sometimes like veal." I don't know if I'd go that far, but after a good deal of mastication it did, ultimately, go down.

Thanks to Aunt Lois, I have had to be game (pun intended) to try any number of things that I probably would not have without her insistence. Among other things, I have picked shot off my plate, learned to ignore the fact that supper looked like Kermit from the waist down, and been educated as to the best way to pull the skin off a catfish. And I am a better person for it.

So here's to mystery. Here's to culinary adventure. And here's to knowing what's on your plate before the blessing is said.

Walking the Social Tightrope

I remember Granny Mac coming home from Eastern Star and saying, "I saw that Minnie Lee, and she didn't say hello, kiss my foot, ner nuthin'!" Snubbed she was, snubbed! The social protocol had not been followed. She had not been acknowledged.

It was easy then to identify when one had been given the brush-off. Social etiquette was clear—in part because there were vastly fewer considerations when tiptoeing one's way through societal folkways and mores and also because the rules were plain. You spoke politely to your friends and acquaintances. You wrote your notes. You brought an appropriate covered dish or small gift. It was easy.

Nowadays the social guidelines are fuzzy at best and downright obscure at worst. There are an infinite number of things to consider.

Is it appropriate to send a thank you email? A thank you tweet? Maybe just a "TY" and a smiley face? Do I follow with a written note? What if I just add a few more exclamation points? It's so tiresome to have to find a stamp.

What if your tweet or post is not replied to? Do your friends suddenly hate you? Are they ignoring you? Was it an affront not to comment on a major life event like what they had for lunch? Am I obligated to comment on everything? What if I never comment? Then I'll be out of the feed/loop/know. Is that really all that bad?

Why was Betty's friend request accepted and not mine? Really now ... Betty? What's wrong with me? It was probably just a glitch in the system. Maybe she meant to click on *my* friend/follow request and hit

Betty's by accident. Who would want to be friends with Betty anyway? Her macaroni and cheese comes out of a box. Tramp.

On the proverbial flip side, am I obligated to be "friends" with more people than my just my real, live, honest-to-goodness friends? Is my boss my friend? Do I really want my boss to know all about my girls' weekend in Destin? Or how about the creepy guy from high school/the mail room/the corner store? I don't want to be his friend, but I don't really want to make him mad either.

Then there are the pictures. There's the party I wasn't invited to but all my friends were or, conversely, I got to go to, but they didn't! Even if I don't post pictures, what if someone else does? Do you even always know when your picture is being taken? And why in the world did Emogene post that shot of me where I was all shiny? My God, what is she trying to do to me? I didn't post the one of her where her bra strap was hanging out … just you wait, Emogene.

And whilst I am sure none of my dear readers are given to philandering, don't dare be somewhere you're not supposed to be with someone you're not supposed to be with! You don't have to be a celebrity nowadays to find your collective mug on the worldwide web *in flagrante delicto*.

Births, deaths, marriage, divorce, adoption, cohabitation, breakup—happy news, sad news, no news … it's all out there. But do you really want to find out about the death of a relative or a friend's divorce right after reading the daily lunch specials posted by the taco truck? What if your boyfriend suddenly changes his status to "it's complicated" when you thought you were fixing to change yours to "engaged?"

And who knew my cousin's brother-in-law's stepdad's girlfriend was the leader of Republicans for Wicca? My aunt took up belly dancing? My great-uncle collects dolls? Was that who I think it was on that float dressed like Carmen Miranda? Should I make mention? Ignore it? Can't wait for Thanksgiving this year!

It really is all too much for the manners-conscious to bear. The slights! The provocations! The ramifications! Where does it all end?

Best to remember the old adage: If you can't say something nice, stay off the internet and come sit by me.

How Are Your Mama and 'Em?

If there is one thing that sets southerners apart from the rest of the country, it has to be our hospitality. Over and over people who are not from here tell me just how nice everyone is, how downright friendly. So much so that it's almost, well, weird.

Drive down any country road, and you will inevitably pass an old truck driven by an old man. If you are good friends or kin, he will wave at you with his whole hand. If he is only slightly acquainted with you, he will cordially lift two fingers from the steering wheel in sort of a half-wave. If you are a stranger, he will still raise his index finger to acknowledge your presence in the world.

But that's down here.

"Don't look anyone in the eye! And don't talk to every person you pass!"

This admonishment came from my friend the first time I visited her in New York. And I have to tell you, it was hard. When you're raised in a place where everybody smiles, waves, and hugs their way through society, it is all but impossible to walk through a throng of city folk, stony-faced and silent, without so much as a nod.

Down here, we ask about your mama and 'em. We go calling. We sit with the sick and sometimes the dead. We hold the baby. We pat your back when you win. We commiserate when you lose. We lend a cup of sugar. We hold the door. We help you raise a big ole barn. We help you raise a little Cain.

And most of the time we do it with a covered dish in tow. Soup, stew, casserole, cake, and/or quickbread—we all have a set of recipes for any particular occasion. After all, everyone knows the best way to raise the spirits is to fill the belly.

Why are southerners like that? Why do we go out of our way to help a perfect stranger? Why do we turn up on the new neighbor's front porch with a basket of muffins?

Because Mama raised us that way. Because it is better to give than to receive. Because it is the right thing to do.

Because we're southerners.

There's Always Room for One More

Brother balances the tinfoil-wrapped plates on his lap while I crank up Mama's big Mercury, even though I'm not quite old enough to drive. The smell of turkey, dressing, and sweet potatoes fills the car. Brother looks a little scared as I mash the pedal to the floor slinging a little driveway gravel as we roar toward town.

He still gives me that same look when I drive.

We've been sent off to deliver plates to those who might otherwise not have a Thanksgiving dinner. Mama's orders. I'd do anything she asked just so I could drive.

But that wasn't the point. And I knew it. I was even a little bit proud that Mama trusted me to take Brother and make the rounds.

One by one we knocked on doors, hugged necks, put the plates on the kitchen table. "Have a happy Thanksgiving," we sang out as we headed off to the next stop. Only when the last plate was in the hands of its recipient did we head home to eat our own dinner.

There was always room for one more at Mama and Daddy's table, and there was always at least one. One who couldn't get home for Thanksgiving. One who had no family. One who had nowhere else to go. And if they couldn't get to the table, well, the table would just have to go to them.

Even if it had to be delivered by a fifteen-year-old girl with a lead foot racing down the road belting out "Holiday" along with Madonna, petrified little brother in tow.

It's hard to believe more than thirty years have passed since Brother and I careened around town windows down and radio up singing about making things better and coming together. Many of the people who once pulled a mismatched chair up to our table have long since passed on. What never dies are the stories they shared.

> We used to travel from community to community for dances. (My grandmother suddenly blushes and giggles like a schoolgirl.)
>
> I thought she was a Hollywood starlet passing through town.
>
> What was that crazy fellow's name? Vidmer? What kind of name is that?
>
> Tell the one about the snake!
>
> There was that time at the hunting camp …
>
> Remember the picnic down by the river?
>
> Play the piano for us! "St. Louis Blues"!
>
> Maybe one song …

and on and on and on.

That's what you get when you pull up that extra chair, the piano bench, the card table, and open your home to an old friend or someone new. Good times. Great memories. Something to really be thankful for—an open mind and an open heart.

After all, there's always room for one more.

Hometraining Has Nothing to Do with Puppies

"A car is useless in New York, essential everywhere else.
The same with good manners." Mignon McLaughlin

Down here, we call it "hometraining." You know—manners, comportment, etiquette, social graces.

I know you all are saying, "Manners schmanners. I can remember which fork to use, please and thank you, ma'am and sir, and all that." But hometraining is *so* much more than knowing the difference between a shrimp fork and a pickle fork or when to wear a dinner jacket.

Hometraining teaches one how to put all who are fortunate enough to be in your company at immediate ease. Hometraining allows one be gracious during difficult times, convivial when the occasion is celebratory, and savvy enough to know the difference. Hometraining prevents one from hollering, "*Awkward!*" when the situation is indeed so. Hometraining teaches one to use "one" as a pronoun.

And while it can be learned, *should* be learned, there are a certain few who sail through polite society with such poise and finesse that they have turned hometraining into societal artistry.

You've seen it—her. She glides into a room, and it seems as though every eye swivels around to fix on her. Everything matches, every hair is in place, and she always knows the exact right thing to say at the exact right time. She can discuss the latest fashion or international affairs or the world record bass with equal aplomb. Her mama obviously devoted many an hour to her social development, but she also has that certain *je ne sais quoi* that just can't be taught.

You've also heard it—them. "Bless her heart. She just has *no home-training*." It is an effort for the southern lady to justify how someone can forget to send a thank-you note, not be able to balance a punch cup and a cake plate, neglect to make proper introductions, or say something coarse such as,like "D'ya mind if I cop a squat." There has to be, there *must* be, some reason to fall so far off the wagon of nicety. No one would consciously act so common, would they?

Why certainly not! It must be that she simply was never taught. *Surely* if she only knew better …

Or if *he* … Gentlemen, hometraining is not just for the ladies. You must have it too. Forget those nouveau feminist protestations and open that door, help her on with her coat, pull out her chair, walk on the street side, and guide and protect her with a touch to her back or elbow. For Pete's sake, carry a hanky.

Please don't attack your plate as if your food may escape back off into the wilderness. Refrain from indelicate scratching and adjusting. Try not to spit too much. Steer the conversation away from money, politics, or religion. Don't wear flip-flops with your dress pants. Learn a clean joke and how to tell it. Don't fight unless you have to.

My friends, hometraining consists of many, many things—some superficial, some not. Some things come naturally; some we must work really, really hard on. But all of these admonitions are born from a common, inordinately important principle best stated by Mrs. Emily Post, who may not be a born southerner but who gets right down to where the goats eat when it comes to etiquette. Take her words to heart.

"Manners are a sensitive awareness of the feelings of others. If you have that awareness, you have good manners, no matter what fork you use."

Steam Table Etiquette

One of the most miraculous inventions ever is the steam table. For those of you not familiar with this giant of gastronomical gadgets, let me explain. The steam table is a long, stainless steel contraption filled with hot water to keep bins of food warm, palatable, and at the ready for the hungry throngs that will pass before its sneeze guard, stomachs rumbling and mouths watering. If you go to the church of Meat and Three,* the steam table is the altar.

What you may not realize is that the steam table commands certain etiquette. There is a method to the madness of providing an endless array of all things fried, casseroled, breaded, broiled, baked, oh … and, of course, steamed. Some establishments are fairly rigid in their expectations that you adhere to the protocol, such as Birmingham, Alabama's, Niki's West, where an ordering faux pas might just get you passed over, but some are more lax, and the nice ladies behind the buffet seem endlessly patient. Nonetheless, you should always be on your best behavior.

What, you may wonder to yourself, does etiquette have to do with a steam table? A lot, actually. There are rules—sometimes written,

---

* What is "meat and three?" It's a meat served with three vegetables on the side. And, yes, macaroni and cheese is a vegetable. So is cornbread dressing. Don't nitpick about food groups and such. Just surrender. You can also get a "meat and two" if you're on a diet or something crazy like that. A "meat and three" can also refer to the restaurant that serves food this way.

sometimes just understood—but rules at any rate that must be followed in order to maintain the integrity and the function of the steam table.

Make sure you are dressed appropriately. If you wish to worship at the Altar of Steam, you must dress for the occasion. Now no one expects you to don your full Sunday-going-to-meeting attire just to get lunch, but you are, after all, out in public and should be suitably clad. I defer to Niki's again for their bold statement on the proper attire posted clearly on a sign at the front door:

TO BE SERVED

MUST BE PROPERLY DRESSED

<u>NO TANK TOPS</u>

<u>NO BARE FEET</u>

<u>NO ROLLERS ON HEAD</u>

Take it to heart. Cover what should be covered, make sure your 'do is done, and head on out for some finger-lickin' good lunch!

Always keep the line moving. No matter how interesting your companions' gossip may be, no matter how much you want to know what happened on *The Young and the Restless*, do not become so enthralled in conversation that you fail to move ahead with the line. The people behind you will become restless, start coughing and shuffling in a veiled attempt to snap you out of your oblivion, and eventually will give you an exasperated tap or nudge. The beauty of the steam table, you see, aside from its ability to provide about a million delicious choices at any given time, is its efficiency. Do not, for any reason, no matter what Wanda did at the bridal shower after mimosas and before petit fours, fail to keep the line moving ever forward.

Plan ahead. A menu will always be posted, somewhere. It is your mission to find said menu and make your choices. If you are lucky, like at Niki's, there will be a menu *and* the line will make several passes in front of the steam table. You should take this opportunity to assess the menu items. When you get to the trays, however, your decision must be made. When you are acknowledged, do not waver. Do not stammer. Proclaim your choices in a clear and concise manner, and then refer to Rule 1. Your plate will find you on down the line when it is ready for you.

Children do not get to choose. The steam table does not constitute window-shopping for food. This is no time for a "teachable moment." Furthermore, all the choices will break a child down faster than the prize counter at Chuck E. Cheese's. No one wants to be in line behind you and little Bitsy when y'all get into a standoff because you want her to have broccoli and all she wants is macaroni and cheese. God forbid it escalates to the point where she throws herself to the floor in a hissy fit. Avoid the embarrassment, the reproachful glances, the raised eyebrows. Tell little Bitsy what she wants ahead of time, get it for her, and keep that line moving!

Get off the phone. The people behind the counter have been there since the early morning. They are hot. They are harried. They will be standing there long after you have finished your coconut pie and third glass of tea. They deserve your attention and respect. Get off the phone, and give it to them. Nothing on that phone is so important you can't take a break to order your meat and three. And if it is life or death, you shouldn't be standing in line at the steam table anyway.

Don't forget to tip. You may think that since you had to stand in line and carry your own plate, you don't have to tip. My friend, you thought wrong. The nice lady who had unloaded your tray, kept your glass full, removed your detritus, and fetched you pepper sauce and extra butter is every bit as deserving of a tip as anyone. Be generous. Be more than generous.

The steam table—a southern institution, a wondrous creation, a meat-and-three miracle. By following just a few itty, bitty rules, common courtesy really, you too can revel all up in it. Just remember to save a slice of pie for me!

Love and Collards

February brings two things to my mind: love and collards.

Love because of the customary celebration of St. Valentine's Day and all things mushy, gushy, sweet, and sentimental. Collards because February is the peak season for this mighty green, my personal favorite of all the greens in the green family. And as I have contemplated love and collards, and believe me there has been some serious cogitation on the matter, I have come to find that the two have much in common.

Collards, like love, can sometimes be sweet and sometimes be salty. The key is to find the perfect balance. If you bring constant contention to the marital table (or the living-in-sin table or the mr.-right-right-now-table), you will create a completely unpalatable situation for your beloved. That is not to say, however, that you should be completely milquetoast and mooney. A dash of salt here and a pinch of sugar there will lead to equilibrium, harmony, happiness.

Collards take a lot of work to get them just right—wash, wash, wash, rinse, rinse, rinse, cut out the stems, check for bad spots, stack the leaves, roll them up, slice, slice, slice. So too does love and marriage. Once you get that ring on your finger, you can't expect to just lie back, eat bonbons, and let the chips of bliss fall where they may. It is a lot of effort to maintain a happy home, and don't let anybody tell you different. But just like a mess of greens, if you are willing to put in the time, effort, and a heaping spoonful of patience, oh, what a sweet reward in the end.

Collards are a tough green, but they can be easily bruised and damaged. You have to treat your collards gently, tenderly, compassion-ately. Even the biggest, toughest outside leaf is in danger of being broken if treated carelessly. Do thoughtless, irreparable damage to your collards, and you will wind up with not so much as a spoonful of potlikker. And then where will you be? Staring at a plate of dry cornbread all by yourself.

Collards ain't nothing but collards no matter how much you try to church them up. You can call them "braised winter greens," you can cut them into a *chiffonade*, you can even try to put them in a gratin or some other such nonsense, but they will still always be just plain collards. Likewise, if your honey pie was a threat to go to the store in a wife-beater and sweatpants, leave his drawers on the bathroom floor, and drink milk straight from the carton before you were married, chances are he will continue to do all those same things once you jump the broomstick. No matter how you try to dress him in Brooks Brothers and Cole Haan, no matter if you douse him in Old Spice and pomade, he'll always be the collard you fell in love with underneath. Don't try to turn him into swiss chard.

Collards are good for you. Collards make you healthy. They provide comfort, make you feel all warm inside, and give you strength to carry on from day to day. Collards should bring nothing but happiness. If your col-lards make you miserable, if your collards make you sad, if your collards are in someone else's pot, well, you might want to consider swiss chard.

So come this Valentine's Day, think of love. Think of collards. I'll have a heaping helping of both, please.

Saturdays Down South

Sometimes you find yourself in a moment that seems cinematic, as if you've been somehow dropped into a movie. But you're not the ingénue. You're the observant extra on the bus stop bench. The one around whom all the activity swirls while you suck on a Big Gulp and try not to stand out. You know that your commentary on the situation at hand will be recorded for all of posterity in the raise of an eyebrow, the subtle widening of the eyes, the purse of your lips. You hope that if you really have been transported into a movie, it's more Wes Anderson and less Quentin Tarantino.

That happens to me a lot. Most recently yesterday. With Husband.

It was a little more than a moment, perhaps fifteen minutes, but in that short time, many stories were told. And that's what I love about living in the South, a place where people of all kinds come together for a short time and with a common goal. They meet in a place where strangers interact, or don't, but where everyone can celebrate a victory together. A place where you'll always be somebody's baby.

Here is a word movie—a short, if you will—about those few minutes from a Saturday down South:

There is little that will spirit Husband away from the television on a football Saturday, but this Saturday, being a slow one in terms of great gridiron challenges, we decide to venture out into the day. We are driven by hunger pangs and a deep hollow feeling that can only be filled by one thing—swine flesh. Not just any old piece of baloney on a cracker can fill a void like that. The only cure is barbecue, preferably pulled with chunks of charred bark and a sauce that makes your mouth fill up with more spit than is ladylike just from the thought of it. There must be dill pickle slices and a white bread bun that goes to mush as it becomes one with the grease. There must be white Styrofoam and a roll of paper towels.

We go to the gittin' place, which today was Saw's Soul Kitchen in Avondale. I make a U-turn to score a parking place right across the street. While many of Saw's neighbors have slicked up the old buildings with chrome, wood, and bright paint, Saw's has done little to improve the outside of its building, and even less on the inside. I like it that way.

We approach the building as the sun plays hide-and-seek with the clouds and a humid breeze with just a scant tease of fall spreads the smoky goodwill of 'cue throughout the neighborhood. A man washes the front window with something that looks like watery Yoohoo. *Sqeeeee-geeee. Squeeee-geeee.* He wipes it clean with his onomatopoetic tool.

We duck past him under the dingy, once-white metal awning. There is a sign on the entry. "Please close door. AC on." We enter. We shut the door behind us. We are in a place now that can only be described as close.

There are about seven tables with mismatched chairs. A couple of them are occupied, one by the front window and one by the wall. A television hangs above the corner table. Most eyes in the place are on it. The University of Alabama is playing. The announcers' voices are muffled, but you can tell when something is happening, even if you aren't watching. The room gets a little quiet, the announcers speak a little faster, a little louder. A man in a white apron hollers, "Go, baby, go!" from the kitchen. One lady answers his call with the only appropriate response there is: "Roll Tide!" There is cheering, both on the television and in the restaurant. Then a commercial.

The back wall is the menu, chalked main items and sides. Smoked chicken. Pork. Catfish. All the usual things one expects when one ventures into this sort of establishment. They have banana pudding. The bathroom is to the right of the menu. You order to the left.

There is a young woman who is standing near the cash register talking on a cell phone. She's staring at the menu, but engrossed in her conversation. She's close enough to the counter that we think she's in line. We hang back, giving her an appropriate amount of space even though we are all in a very small one. I catch her eye. She motions us to go ahead. She keeps talking. And staring. We go ahead.

There is no one at the register. The man in the white apron stands at a prep station with a row of white Styrofoam in front of him. With his right hand, he scoops up a big spoonful of greens, and with two quick jerks of his wrist, sends the potlikker back into the pot before the greens get sent to the go-box. His left hand grabs several buns that get set out … one, two, three … down the line, waiting for their pickles, which are soon to come. His eyes still on the television, his hands and arms seem to have a mind of their own, filling the orders while he follows the game.

A harried woman comes to the register. She has a tattoo on her neck. It is in all fancy script, part black, part bright red. I have to resist the urge to lean across the counter to read it. Her eyebrows have been plucked razor thin. Black eyeliner, smeared from a day in the sweaty kitchen, settles into lines that could be called laugh, but probably aren't. She looks at the television.

"Hep ya, baby?" For those of you not familiar with the vernacular of the South, she means "May I please take your order?"

We order and get a ticket and two Styrofoam cups. Our number is 166. Drinks are on the same counter. We opt for tea, unsweet with a splash of sweet. Now there is sweet tea, and there is *sweet tea*. The latter seems to run from the spigot a little slower. It will make your teeth ache. You might have to wash it down with a glass of water because sugar syrup will make you feel good, but it won't quench a thirst. I know this sweet tea is *that* sweet tea from the few drops I mixed with the dastardly unsweet. The combination is perfect.

We sit at a table by the window. "Roll Tide" is behind Husband. She is licking her fingers. The door is behind me. I know the sign works because everyone who comes in slams the door. Not in a rude way. In the way you have to slam a door swollen by humidity. We sit and wait. Wait for 166.

The referee's whistle is shrill. "Pork up!" "Drop some catfish!" "Roll Tide!" The window washer is now taking out the trash, a big sackful of greasy napkins, melted ice, Styrofoam. The smell of garbage mixes with the other scents in these cramped quarters—vinegar, smoke, Clorox. He maneuvers through the tables, past the line, which now snakes almost to the door.

There is a man in camel-colored wingtips. He is tall and slim. The creases in his pants could cut you. His shirt is starched with heavy starch. Niagra. He is alone. His eyes are on the television.

There is another couple who are approaching middle age. They order and sit by the drink fountain. She stares one way, he another. They don't speak. They don't smile. They don't look at one another or at anyone else. They don't even look at the television.

The girl on the cell phone has ordered and is waiting near me. She's still talking. "I told her he was sorry, but she wouldn't listen." She seems filled with righteous indignation, exasperated. I understand. Some people are just sorry. Some people never listen.

A young woman with two little children sits at the next table down. The little girl is probably three, the little boy not quite a year. She lays the little boy across her lap and starts to take his pants off. I'm a mother. I know what's coming. She shimmies his little pants off, glances around the room, and gives them a quick sniff. Unsatisfied, she puts them on the table. She takes him by the ankle and holds one leg up and takes a tentative peek into the diaper. She looks momentarily relieved, until the little boy reaches out and grabs a handful of his sister's hair. The little girl shrieks. The little boy hangs on. The mother tries to pry his fingers loose. Babies are stronger than you think. She looks tired.

I look at Husband. He's watching the game too. Engrossed like most everyone else. The referee's whistle shrills in short staccatos. "Order up!" says the man in the apron. "One sixty-six one sixty-six!" sings the lady from behind the counter. "One sixty-six to go!"

Husband holds our cups while I claim our white plastic sack filled with white Styrofoam containers. We pick our way back through the tables, through the line, and out the door. We close it firmly behind us.

As we walk across the street, I can still hear the whistles, the cheering. I hear a train in the distance. I imagine that the credits are rolling. The end.

Acknowledgments

I'd like to thank William Dahlberg, Anastasia Ferrell, and Krista Rataj for their eagle eyes, criticism, and ideas. Without your help, the book you hold in your hands would still be a dream in my heart. Thank you to Javacia Harris Bowser and all the ladies of See Jane Write for your guidance and encouragement. And thank you to all y'all who've read my blog, Folkways Nowadays, over the years and shared your own stories with me. Your interest and enthusiasm has been my constant inspiration.

About the Author

Audrey McDonald Atkins grew up in the Oil Capital of Alabama, Citronelle, and spent her childhood roaming through the piney woods, swimming in creeks, and rambling about her small town taking in the sights and sounds of the Deep South and storing them away.

And from the time she could barely see over the space bar to hack out her own weekly newspaper on a manual typewriter to writing her popular southern culture blog, Folkways Nowadays, Audrey's been sharing her funny, poignant, and down-home stories and essays about life in the South.

From her parents and grandparents to the men who congregated in the police station and gossiped to the eccentric characters who worked along Main Street, each and every person still lives in Audrey's memory frozen in time just as they were in the '70s. It's these ghosts of bygone days that shine through the pages that Audrey writes.

Audrey ultimately made her way to the big city of Birmingham after graduating from the University of Montevallo, where she earned a BA in English. While she currently lives in the city and sometimes eats sushi and drinks craft cocktails, her Mayberry-like childhood still gives Audrey a unique and often hilarious outlook on the South and our world.

Edwards Brothers Inc.
Ann Arbor MI. USA
May 10, 2018